crest rail, or bow

arm rail (steam-bent)

oval seat

24

The Windsor Style in America
Volume II

THE

WINDSOR STYLE

in AMERICA

Volume II

A Continuing Pictorial Study of the History and Regional Characteristics of the Most Popular Furniture Form of Eighteenth-Century America

1730-1840

By Charles Santore

Thomas M. Voss, Editor
Photographs by Bill Holland

RUNNING PRESS
Philadelphia, Pennsylvania

Canadian representatives: General Publishing Co., Ltd.,
30 Lesmill Road, Don Mills, Ontario M3B 2T6
International representatives: Worldwide Media Services, Inc.,
115 East 23rd Street, New York, NY 10010

9 8 7 6 5 4 3 2 1
Digit on the right indicates the number of this printing.

Library of Congress Cataloging-in-Publication Data
(Revised for volume 2)
Santore, Charles.
The Windsor style in America.
Includes bibliographical references and index.
Contents: [1] A pictorial study of the history and regional
characteristics of the most popular furniture form of 18th-century
America, 1730–1830—v. 2. A continuing pictorial study of the history and
regional characteristics of the most popular furniture form of
eighteenth-century America, 1730–1840.
1. Furniture—United States—History—18th century. 2. Decoration and
ornament—Windsor style. I. Voss, Thomas M., 1945–   . II. Title.
NK2406.S36   749.214   81-10682

ISBN 0–89471–137–7 (Lib. Bdg.)

ISBN 0–89471–551–8 (Cloth)

Photographs: By Bill Holland—pages ii, 26–30, 34–39; figures 1–4, 6–8, 10–16A, 18, 19, 23–34,
36, 39, 42–44, 46, 47, 49–61, 63–68, 70–85, 87–90, 93–110, 112, 114–117, 119–122, 124, 126,
128–138, 141–144, 146, 147, 149, 150, 152–154, 156–164, 166–170, 172–175, 177, 179–184, 187,
189, 190, 194–197, 199–201, 203–205, 208, 210–213A, 216–224, 226, 228–231, 234, 235,
238–245, 247–265, 268, 270; pages 242, 243 (lower l. and r.), 244 (center and lower r.), 245
(upper l. and r.), 246 (upper l. and upper r.), 247 (r.), 248 (r.), 249 (l.), 250 (l.), 251 (r.), 252 (l.
and lower r.), 253, 254 (upper l.), 255 (r.), 256, 257 (lower l. and r.), 258, 259 (l. and upper r.),
260 (l. and lower r.), 261 (center), 262 (upper r.), 263 (r.), 264 (lower l., upper and lower r.), 265,
266 (center and lower r.), 267 (lower l.), 268 (upper and center r.), 269. Photographs for figure
40 and for page 247 (center) copyright © 1987 by Luigi Pellettieri. Wayne Pratt's photographs
are courtesy of John J. Courville. Photograph of Oliver Swan label, page 264, reprinted from *The
Folk Tradition: Early Arts and Crafts of the Susquehanna Valley* compiled by Richard Barons,
copyright © 1982 by The Roberson Center, Binghamton, N.Y.

Drawings on pages 17–24 copyright © 1981, 1987 by Charles Santore
Cover design by Toby Schmidt
Typography by Deputy Crown, Camden, NJ
Display type by Composing Room, Philadelphia, PA
Printed by South Seas International Press, Ltd., Hong Kong

This book may be ordered by mail from the publisher. Please add $2.00
postage and handling for each copy. *But try your bookstore first!*

Running Press Book Publishers
125 South Twenty-Second Street
Philadelphia, PA 19103

To Olenka

Contents

Foreword

When I first read *The Windsor Style in America*—the book by Charles Santore that preceded the present volume—I was delighted. I felt that never before had a writer done such an interesting, thorough job of recounting the history and analyzing the design of a single form of early American furniture.

Now we have *The Windsor Style, Volume II*, and once again I am delighted.

This book, a comprehensive supplement to the first, is not so much a history of the Windsor style as it is a compendium of regional comparisons and influences. Santore shows us hundreds of examples of Windsor chairs from various regions and points up their similarities and differences; he shows how similar pieces from different regions and from within the same region may have influenced each other; and he discusses the aesthetic qualities of each one.

Santore also poses some thoughtful questions about Windsors: Why were most writing-arm Windsors made in Connecticut? Why were fan-back Windsors produced in quantity in Pennsylvania but infrequently in New York? Why was the continuous-arm chair so popular in New York but not in Pennsylvania? Those questions and others are answered intelligently and perceptively.

This informative, authoritative book is one that collectors, curators, and dealers will treasure, not only for ready reference but for the pure pleasure of browsing through its handsome pages.

Dr. Robert Bishop
Director
Museum of American Folk Art
New York City

Preface

Not long after I delivered to Running Press the final manuscript, photographs, and drawings for my first book, *The Windsor Style in America 1730–1830*, I began to feel another book coming on! The primary reason was that Windsor chairs I had never seen before kept turning up—chairs I felt should have been included in the book.

My editor, Tom Voss, and my publishers, Lawrence and Stuart Teacher, said, "Stop! No more! *Fini!* You've made your point!"

I reluctantly agreed. But then I would discover yet another new example and say to myself, "Look at that chair. It has an arm support (or a comb-piece, or a leg) that I've never seen before. Windsor collectors should know about this."

The variety of chairs seemed endless, the list of chairmakers grew, and new variations of styles kept emerging.

The opportunity to organize a Windsor loan exhibition for the University Hospital Antiques Show in Philadelphia in 1982 brought me into contact with yet another group of fine Windsors, many never before seen publicly. And the publication of *The Windsor Style in America* began to prove very rewarding to me in a way I had not anticipated: until then, I had had to ferret out as best I could most of the Windsor forms and related information I compiled. After the book's publication, collectors, dealers, and antiquarians began sending me photos of Windsors and information they thought would interest me, sharing what they knew as well as asking for my opinions.

Far and away, though, the majority of the letters and phone calls were about forms of Windsors that did not appear in *The Windsor Style*, or in Wallace Nutting's *American Windsors*, or in Thomas Ormsbee's *The Windsor Chair*. The only response I could make to these inquiries was to write a new book about it all—the book you are holding in your hands.

Nutting, Ormsbee, and I—in attempting to cover the evolution, variety, and basic types of Windsors—had been forced to select examples of chairs that emphasized striking differences among Windsors from period to period and from region to region. In order to show these differences graphically, we had to skip over the many similarities and the more subtle differences that could fill in the gaps of our Windsor vocabulary. In this volume I have included many Windsors that are similar in turning patterns, construction, and general impact. I believe that in doing so I have been able to paint more clearly a realistic picture of the Windsor panorama in America.

The more American Windsors I see, the more I am convinced that American chairmakers followed the English tradition more closely than previously believed. In England, particular types or styles of chairs are frequently named after the places of their production. Thus we have Yorkshire, Lancashire, Mendelsham, and High Wycombe Windsors—to name a few.

I've noted in *The Windsor Style* that virtually every type of American Windsor, with the interesting exception of the continuous-arm chair, was first produced in England, and there seems to be universal agreement that the first American Windsors were influenced by the English products. But then—so goes the common wisdom—our own ingenuity took over.

I'm now convinced that the practice of identifying a particular style or type of Windsor with a particular city or region was as common here as it was in England. This notion has probably been overlooked because, with the exception of the "Philadelphia chair," we did not *name* our chairs after their places of origin. But if we were not as quick as the English to speak for our chairs, the chairs will speak for themselves. And what they tell us is that there is a pattern in Windsors produced in different regions, from Maine to Virginia, between 1730 and the mid-nineteenth century.

Why does one very prolific and sophisticated center of Windsor chairmaking—New York City—produce virtually no comb-back or fan-back chairs, types already made popular by another prolific chairmaking center—Philadelphia? On the other hand, why does Philadelphia produce no continuous-arm chairs—a type that originated in New York City and influenced Windsor design in most of the colonies? Why do at least 60 to 70 percent of all Windsor writing-arm chairs come from a single region—Connecticut—and the majority of those from a single shop—that of E. B. Tracy?

The evidence seems to indicate that chairmaking centers were content with, and probably proud of, the Windsor styles they sold the most of, and that they simply conceded the other types to their respective centers. Thus, although a style was seldom named after the place of its greatest production and popularity, it went without saying that its place of origin was synonymous with its design.

Such patterns are most evident in the large, urban chairmaking centers. The influence of these centers on their neighboring communities might, in turn, spread to another small community that had already been exposed to yet another chairmaking center, and so on. The end result was stylistic specialization in the urban centers and stylistic proliferation in the provinces.

By studying the similarities and differences among Windsors, one can see how aware American craftsmen were of developments around them, and how quickly they incorporated external influences into their own Windsor vocabulary. It is only by studying the products of these prolific craftsmen that we can understand their intentions, aesthetic sense, business sense, and their attitude toward their craft.

Birth, death, and marriage records, bills of lading, street directories, and advertisements—all of these are important in helping us to understand the Windsor story in America. But those documents notwithstanding, the most revealing document of all is the product—the Windsor chair itself.

As much as possible, I have tried in this book to let the chairs speak for themselves, allowing their own organic development to dictate the organization and content of the book. I hope that this format will be another valuable tool for collectors, dealers, auctioneers, and Windsor scholars.

CHARLES SANTORE

Acknowledgments

I learned, during my experience with the first volume of this book, that it is impossible to produce a book of this type without the interest and help of a great many people. So it comes as no surprise that the present volume has also been a joint effort, and I would sincerely like to acknowledge the support, concern, and assistance of those individuals who contributed their time, expertise, and collections in making this book a reality.

First, I would like to thank Tom Voss and Bill Holland for their collaboration on this project. I have come to rely on their vision and insight, and this book, like our last, is better because of their participation. More important, we are still friends.

A special thanks is due to Dr. Robert Bishop for his interest, concern, and enthusiasm for this project.

Many knowledgeable collectors and Windsor-lovers graciously opened their collections to me, unhesitatingly offering their cooperation and advice. For their invaluable assistance, I would like to thank Roy and Carol Allen, Claude and Alvan Bisnoff, H. Richard Dietrich, Jr., William K. du Pont, Steven and Helen Kellogg, Don and Joan Mayoras, Mr. and Mrs. John C. Price, and Tom and Nancy Tafuri.

I am extremely grateful for the expertise and unflagging support of Sam Bruccoleri, James and Nancy Glazer, Wayne Pratt, and David Schorsch. They are always on the alert for new Windsor discoveries, and they have my respect, admiration, and deepest thanks.

I would like to include a very special mention of my gratitude to my publishers, Lawrence and Stuart Teacher, whose personal interest in early American furniture and Windsors in particular was so evident in publishing *The Windsor Style* and which is now reaffirmed in this book; and to Elizabeth Zozom and the entire design department at Running Press: I'm very proud of our relationship. To Nancy Steele, my editor at Running Press whose guidance and careful scrutiny in every detail of this book was so critically important, my deepest respect and gratitude.

I have always felt fortunate to be so close to Independence National Historical Park. Having access to its superb collection of Philadelphia Windsors has been a wonderful opportunity, and I owe a debt of gratitude to all the staff of INHP. I would like to thank particularly Park Superintendent Hobart Caywood, Chief of Museum Operations John C. Milley, Supervisory Curator Doris Fanelli, Assistant Curators Jane Coulter and Robert Ganini, and staff members Ricardo Hutchinson and Gloria McLean.

For their valuable assistance and generosity I am deeply grateful to Lynne Anderson, Rosemary Beck and Ed Rogers, Barry Blum of Blum's Antiques, Charles E. Bolton of Federation Antiques, Richard A. Bourne Co., Inc., Philip H. Bradley Antiques, James Brooks, Tom Brown Antiques,

Richard Chalfant, Skip and Lee Ellen Chalfant, Richard Champlin, Marianne Clark, The Clokeys, Barry Cohen, Michael Cook, Suzanne Courcier and Robert Wilkens, Elizabeth R. Daniel, Charles G. Dorman, Hazel Douglass, Nancy Druckman, Joseph Dumas, Howard and Kathy Feldman, Burton and Helaine Fendelman, Amy Finkel, Kenneth Finkel, Morris Finkel, Paul and Rita Flack, Kyle and Doris Fuller, Frank R. Gaglio and Kathleen Molner, Albert F. Gamon, Elizabeth R. Gamon, Ralph Giguere, Peter and Janie Gross, Tom and Karen Helm, Don and Trish Herr, Marjorie Hooper, Charles Miller and Charlotte Hornberger, Charles W. Huntress, William C. Jennens, Victor and Joan Johnson, Elizabeth Kannan, Maribeth Keene and Wayne Pratt Antiques, Mr. and Mrs. Gary Koenig, Leigh Keno, Leslie Keno, Doug and Kendra Krienke, Ed and Audrey Kornowski, Richard F. Kozar, Allan and Joan Lehner, Anthony Leone, Bernard & S. Dean Levy, Sarah Lippincott of Lippincott Antiques, Mr. and Mrs. Gary W. Lipton, Michael McCue and Mike Rothstein, Chris and Corinne Machmer, Kenneth and Ida Manko, Mr. and Mrs. Craig Mayor, Christine Meadows, Dr. and Mrs. Donald McHarl, John Mecray, Alan Miller, Kathleen Mulhern, Charles Muller, John C. Newcomer, Sam Pennington, M. M. Pernot, Eugene Pettinelli, Michael Pillagalli, Frank and Barbara Pollack, David Pottinger, Deborah McCracken Rebuck, Frank Rentschler, Gregory and Barbara Reynolds, Marguerite Riordan, William Schwind, Jr., Antiques, Mr. and Mrs. Steven Score, William Stahl, Lita Solis-Cohen, Barbara and Chuck Soltis, Robert Stallfort, Charles Sterling, Mason Stewart, Tom Strofelt, Howard Szmolko, Nancy and Alan Tessler, Robert Trent, Mrs. Jo Ann Wagner, Mark and Kathy Winchester, Edwin Wolf, Stephanie Wood, and Richard Worth. Wayne Pratt's photographs are courtesy of John J. Courville.

I am also grateful for the assistance of "The Arts and Antiques Review" of the *Newtown Bee;* The John Bartram Association; The Burlington County Historical Society; The Chester County Historical Society; Christie's; Colonial Williamsburg; The Concord Antiquarian Society; The Dietrich American Foundation; The Library Company of Philadelphia; Ludens, Inc.; *The Maine Antique Digest;* The Metropolitan Museum of Art; Mount Vernon; The Mount Vernon Ladies Association; The Museum of Early Southern Decorative Arts; The New Hampshire Historical Society; The Pennsylvania Historical Society; David and Marjorie Schorsch, Inc., The Redwood Library and Atheneum; Sotheby's; Waynesborough; Whistler Gallery, Inc.; The Peter Wenz Farmstead; The Henry Francis du Pont Winterthur Museum; The Yale University Art Gallery.

To all of the aforementioned, I am deeply indebted. Thank you.

A Portfolio of Drawings

1.   Philadelphia and New England bamboo-turned legs and stretchers.
     Top to bottom: medial stretcher, Boston, 1790–1796; medial and side stretcher, Philadelphia, 1780–1793.
     Left to right: rear leg, Philadelphia, 1780–1793; front leg, Boston, 1790–1796.

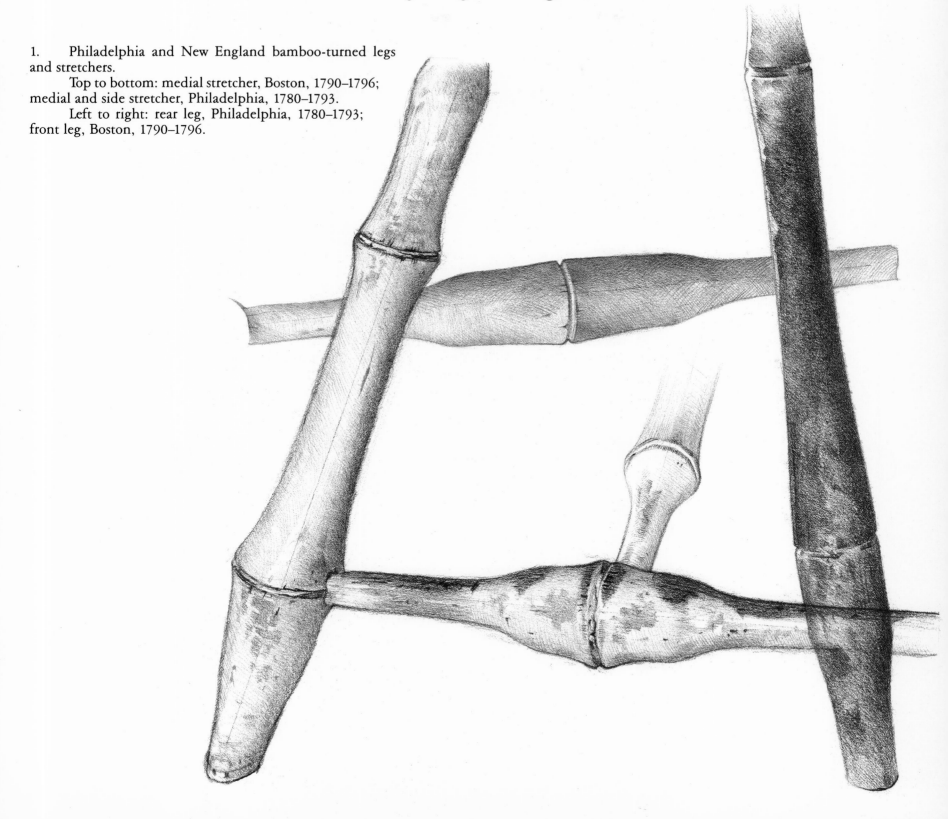

2.   New England and Philadelphia leg and back
post turnings for children's fan-back side chairs.
    Left to right: front leg and back post, Lisbon,
Connecticut, 1790–1800; back post and front leg,
Philadelphia, 1765–1780.

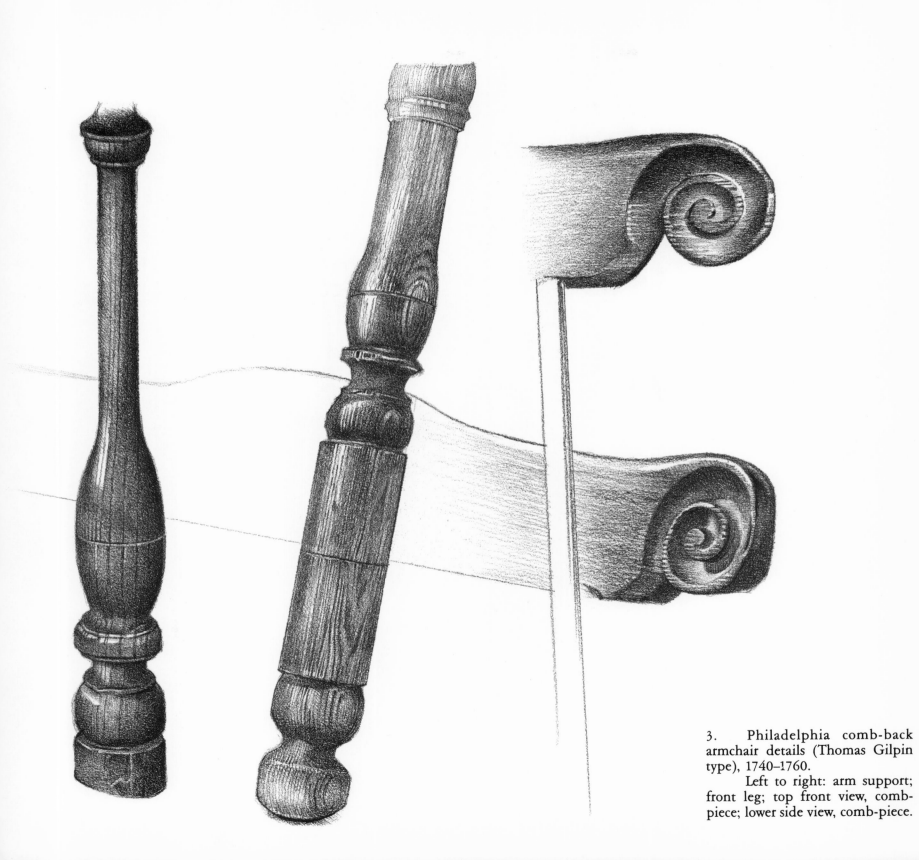

3. Philadelphia comb-back armchair details (Thomas Gilpin type), 1740–1760.
Left to right: arm support; front leg; top front view, comb-piece; lower side view, comb-piece.

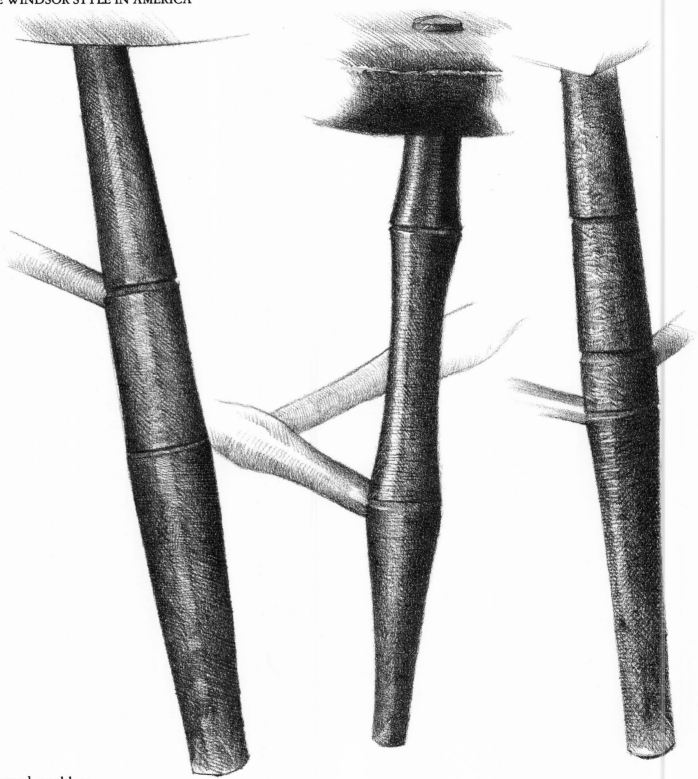

4.   New England bamboo-turned stool legs.
      Left to right: box stretcher type, Massachusetts, 1800–1820;
medial stretcher type, New England, 1790–1800; box stretcher type,
New England, 1800–1820.

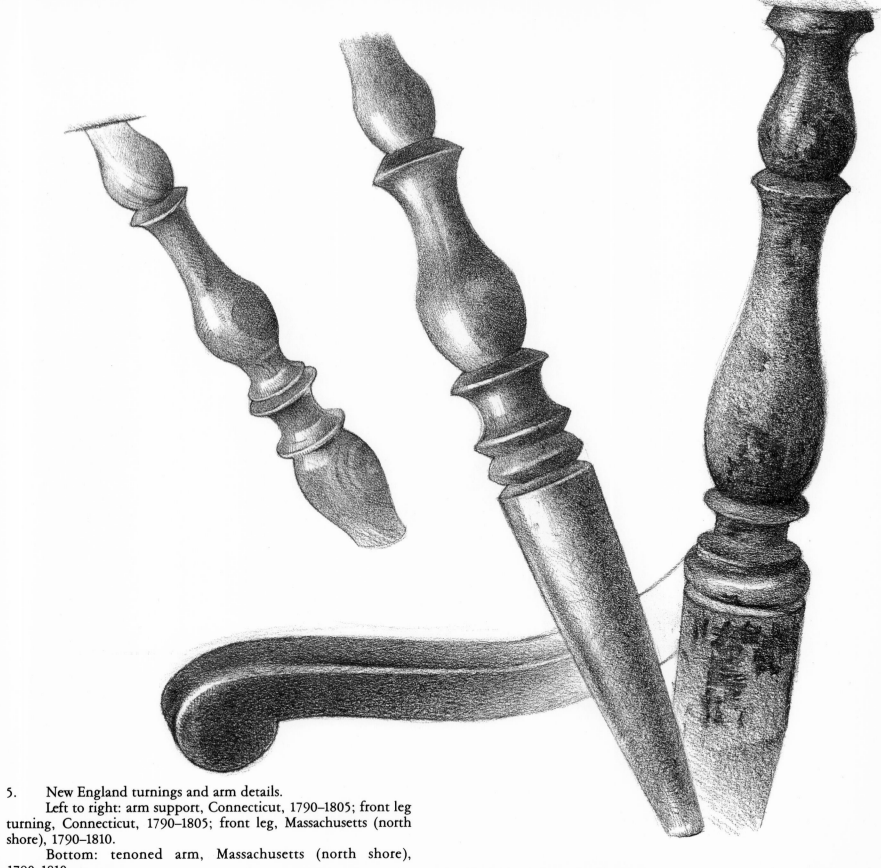

5. New England turnings and arm details.
Left to right: arm support, Connecticut, 1790–1805; front leg turning, Connecticut, 1790–1805; front leg, Massachusetts (north shore), 1790–1810.
Bottom: tenoned arm, Massachusetts (north shore), 1790–1810.

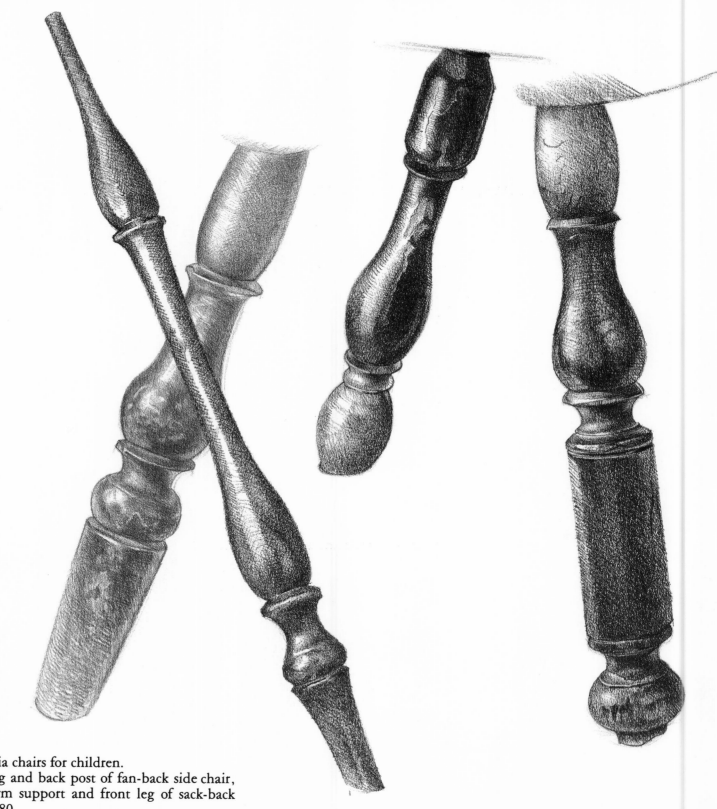

6.   Details of Philadelphia chairs for children.
      Left to right: front leg and back post of fan-back side chair,
Philadelphia, 1765–1780; arm support and front leg of sack-back
chair, Philadelphia, 1765–1780.

7.   Philadelphia Windsor chair details.

Top to bottom: comb-piece, 1745–1770; comb-piece, 1765–1780; handhold of steam-bent arm, 1740–1770; knuckle handhold and turned arm support, 1765–1780; arm and crest rail of low-back chair, 1750–1770.

Lower left to right: medial stretcher, 1740–1760; leg, 1765–1780; leg, 1745–1760; arm support, 1745–1760.

© Charles Santore 1981

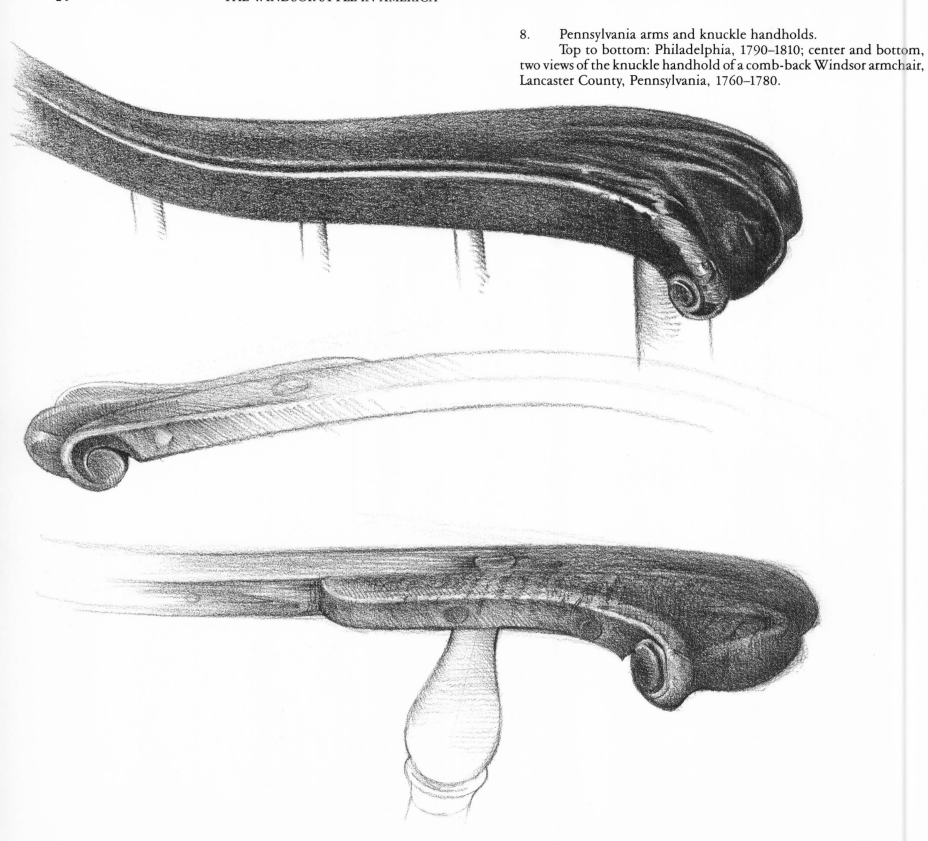

8.   Pennsylvania arms and knuckle handholds.
Top to bottom: Philadelphia, 1790–1810; center and bottom, two views of the knuckle handhold of a comb-back Windsor armchair, Lancaster County, Pennsylvania, 1760–1780.

A Study of Windsor Surfaces

Plate I.   Portrait of a mother and child, probably by Jacob Maentel; probably Lancaster County, Pennsylvania; early nineteenth century. Watercolor on paper. 10″ × 15″. (Barry Cohen)

The paint colors of the Windsor chairs shown in this picture—apple green with yellow, and some red, decoration—were very fashionable in the first quarter of the nineteenth century. Note that, although the chairs have been painted to match, the high chair does not have arrow-shaped spindles; thus the chairs were probably not part of a set.

Plate II. Armchair. Originally painted dark green, this is a good example of a Windsor chair dating from the third quarter of the eighteenth century that was "updated" in the early nineteenth century with the same fashionable combination of apple-green paint with red, blue, and gilt striping and decoration seen in Plate I. The flaking here and there of the newer paint, exposing the original paint, creates a marvelous surface quality. (Also see figure 76.)

Plate III.   Armchair. While this master-piece of Philadelphia Windsor chair-making of the 1765–1780 period has a coat of late eighteenth- or early nineteenth-century reddish-brown grain paint over its original green paint, the chair as it stands is in untouched condition. Since absolutely nothing would be gained by attempting to remove the second coat of paint by dry-scraping, the chair should be left exactly as it is, with its undisturbed paint history intact. (Also see figures 16 and 16A.)

Plate IV.   Armchair. I have seen many early Windsors with paint histories like that of this chair: nineteenth-century red paint over earlier nineteenth-century buff, over the original eighteenth-century green. As is common in these examples, the hickory spindles, which do not hold paint very well, are pleasingly mottled, revealing the different levels and colors of paint.

On such a chair, the patina becomes as important as the structure, making the piece a rare—and, from the collector's point of view, exciting—historical document. However, while this chair is very desirable, it is slightly less so than the previous two examples because it has three, rather than two, coats of paint. (Also see figure 3.)

Plate V. Candlestand. So often we speak of "original green paint" on Windsor furniture. Here is what it comes to look like when it is completely undisturbed for more than 200 years (in this case, laid over a salmon-color ground). For a piece of Windsor furniture to have survived so long in this pristine condition—without having been overpainted—is remarkably rare. (Also see figure 249.)

30

Plate VI. Armchair. The yellows used to paint Windsors were usually soft in tone—ochres or straw colors, for example. This fine and typical rod-back of about 1800, with its original cadmium yellow and black ringing, is almost startlingly bright. The color seems perfectly appropriate for a bamboo-turned Windsor and certainly brings the chair to life. (Also see figure 162.)

Plate VII. High chair. Here is one of those instances when a second coat of early paint—in this case, over the original green—makes a piece more interesting and exciting than it would have been had it been left in its original color.

While this is a well-proportioned sack-back high chair with good bamboo turnings, it is not of the best style. Yet its second coat of nineteenth-century yellow paint with white, ringed with white and red, makes this piece sing. This is an excellent example of how important a bright paint history is to a successful Windsor statement. (Also see figure 231.)

Plate VIII.   Pair of side chairs. Massachusetts, 1790–1810.   Early nineteenth-century mustard-yellow paint over the original green paint. (Collection of David A. Schorsch)

Additional examples of Windsors that have been enhanced by a second coat of paint, these eighteenth-century fan-backs now sport a top coat of bright nineteenth-century yellow paint over the original green. Painted this way, these chairs have a more graphic architecture.

Plate IX.   Armchair. Probably South Windham, Connecticut; 1796–1805. Probably by Amos Denison Allen (it descended in the Amos Denison Allen family). Original blue paint. Crest rail, spindles, and arms, hickory; arm supports and seat, butternut; legs and stretchers, maple. SW 19¾″, SD 15″, SH 16½″, OH 33″. (Collection of David A. Schorsch)

Many of the Windsor chairs known to have been made by Amos Denison Allen were originally painted black with gilt decoration. Probably made by Allen, this chair is a rare find because it has its original blue paint and has never been overpainted.

Plate X. Armchair. This beautifully proportioned Rhode Island continuous-arm chair is about as fine and graceful a piece of Windsor furniture as one could hope to see.

When found, the chair had been overpainted with black and striped decoration, probably of mid-nineteenth-century vintage. Fortunately, the black paint had thoroughly dried out and was literally falling off in spots. What was emerging beneath it was a coat of early nineteenth-century teal-blue paint over the original eighteenth-century green.

In this case, the place to stop removing the paint was obvious. The blue paint was in excellent condition and would never separate from the original green as easily as the black paint separated from the blue. There would be no point in going to the trouble of removing the blue paint anyway, because the chair is wonderful just as it is! (Also see figure 160.)

Plate XI. Side chair. Dry-scraping—usually done with a spoon or a dull knife—is a tedious process, yet it is the only tried-and-true method of removing old crystallized paint from a Windsor chair without disturbing the undercoats.

In this photo, we see the results of dry-scraping a coat of early twentieth-century black paint from an upholstered Philadelphia bow-back side chair. The results are quite dramatic: the original white paint, mellowed by time, has been revealed, and the bamboo turnings can now be seen and appreciated. Note the splotches of black paint over the original white still in evidence on the underside of the seat where the legs are socketed. This is a good place to look when trying to determine the paint history of a Windsor chair. (Also see figure 120.)

Plate XII.   Here we see a continuation of the dry-scraping process on the bow and spindles of the chair pictured in Plate XI. On the bow, or crest rail, you can see that where the black paint has already been removed, not much original white paint remains. Close examination reveals that the white paint had been worn away before the chair was painted black. Since the raw oak of the bow was exposed, the black paint was absorbed by the open wood grain, making removal of the black paint extremely difficult. The spindles are a different matter: most of the original white paint was still intact when the chair was overpainted black. The paint bond was weak, and the black paint can now be easily chipped and scraped away.

Plate XIII.   A detail of the wonderfully original crest rail of figure 179 is shown here. The chair retains its original early nineteenth-century brown paint.

Note how the paint is worn along the top of the crest rail, exposing the wood beneath—a telltale sign of age. Such areas of exposed wood on painted Windsors should never be touched up. They are imperfections, yes, but the various smooth spots, bare spots, cracks, scrapes, and scratches are an integral part of the character of a venerable old Windsor. They add up to patina, not just paint color. After all, 200 years ago brown paint was not much different from brown paint today; what's important is how and where the years have affected that paint.

On the other hand, a chair with paint that is crazed on every inch of its surface would be unnatural: one would have to suspect that the "patina" had been manufactured. Similarly, if the quality of the wear were exactly the same on all the chair's surfaces, one would have to check carefully to make certain that the wear had not been faked.

Plate XIV.   The ear of a Connecticut fan-back side chair is shown in this detail. Instead of carved volutes, the ears have a rosette pattern—a kind of stylized floral carving common to Connecticut furniture. Note how, due to use and age, the high spots on the carving have been worn through the paint to the bare wood beneath. Note, too, that the original black paint is thickest and most crazed in the low spots of the carving. When it was first applied, the paint served to decorate, unify, and protect the piece. With time, however, the paint on a piece of early furniture becomes part of its architecture, and the changes in the color and texture of the paint begin to explain and emphasize the piece's form. (Also see figure 61.)

Plate XV. Armchair. A remarkable miniature Windsor chair only 7¼″ tall, this piece retains its original green paint with gilt decoration on the crest rail, front edge of the seat, and turnings. The paint decoration has been scaled down to match the scale of the construction, making the chair a completely successful miniature. (Also see figure 245.)

COMB-BACK

~

CHAIRS

CHAPTER ONE

The comb-back chair is almost certainly the earliest style of Windsor produced in America and is synonymous with Philadelphia. The form probably saw the light of day in that city circa 1730 and was fully realized by 1750. During the 1750–1790 period, the comb-back accounted for a substantial part of Philadelphia Windsor production. But even in Philadelphia, the comb-back seems to have been favored by only a handful of shops, judging by the relative frequency with which these branded and stylistically identifiable examples turn up.

If Philadelphia was the hub of comb-back Windsor chairmaking, its outlying areas were the spokes. For example, many marvelous, highly stylized comb-backs have come out of Lancaster County, Pennsylvania, as well as Chester, Berks, and Bucks counties. Wilmington, Delaware, produced comb-backs, but these chairs are heavily influenced stylistically by the Philadelphia product.

In major chairmaking centers outside the Philadelphia area, very few comb-backs were produced, the other makers apparently choosing not to compete with Philadelphia makers. The two significant exceptions are the cross-stretcher comb-backs in the English taste made in Newport, Rhode Island, and the much smaller comb-backs with long, tapering legs from various areas of Connecticut. The Hartford area produced quite a number of small comb-backs, generally attributable to John Wadsworth during the 1793–1796 period, but the great Connecticut Windsor-making dynasty headed by E. B. Tracy seems to have made few comb-back chairs. New York chairmakers ignored the form in favor of sack-backs, bow-backs, and continuous-arm chairs. And coastal Massachusetts makers seem to have preferred the fan-back armchair to the comb-back type.

The comb-back form is powerful, classic, and difficult to surpass. Some of the finest American Windsors ever produced were made as comb-backs.

1. Armchair. Philadelphia, 1740–1750. Branded T. GILPIN under seat pommel. Early nineteenth-century black paint over the original red paint. Crest rail, oak; spindles, hickory; arms, possibly ash; arm supports, chestnut; seat, poplar; legs, oak or chestnut; stretchers, hickory or chestnut. SW 21″, SD 15″, SH 15½″, OH 40½″. (Privately owned)

Thomas Gilpin (1700–1766) is the earliest Windsor maker whose branded chairs have survived. Indeed, the chairs of no other maker of the early period seem to have been branded. Thus branded Gilpin chairs are a rarity, and this one is rarer still because of its relatively small size. Still, the chair has all the Gilpin characteristics, among them: ears whose contour does not rise at the ends; a comb-piece that is thick on the bottom, allowing the ears to be deeply carved; arm supports with urn-shaped turnings at the top; two short spindles under each arm; and a decoratively turned medial stretcher. Note, too, that the medial stretcher is not socketed in the center of the side stretchers but is "stepped back," a feature of the earliest Philadelphia comb-backs as well as of low-backs.

1

NOTE: In this book, dimensions are given in inches and are abbreviated as SW (seat width), SD (seat depth), SH (seat height), and OH (overall height).

2.   Armchair. Philadelphia, 1740–1750. Dark reddish-brown paint over the original green paint. Crest rail, probably oak; arms and arm supports, ash; spindles, hickory; seat, pine; legs and stretchers, chestnut. SW 24″, SD 16″, SH 17¼″, OH 45″. (James and Nancy Glazer)

While not branded as is figure 1, this chair has all the Gilpin characteristics. The chair never had scrolled handholds, which gives it a rather English feeling.

3.   Armchair. Philadelphia, 1750–1770. Nineteenth-century dark red paint over a buff-color ground, over the original green paint. Crest rail and arms, oak; spindles, hickory; arm supports, legs, and stretchers, maple; seat, poplar. SW 24½″, SD 16¾″, SH 17″, OH 42½″. (Also see color plate IV.) (James and Nancy Glazer)

This is a typical, classic, early Philadelphia comb-back. Noteworthy features include its scrolled ears with two full spirals; nine untapered spindles; three short spindles under each arm; a steam-bent arm rail with scrolled handholds; a medial stretcher in the Queen Anne style; and ball feet (with some loss on this particular chair).

4. Armchair. Philadelphia, 1750–1770. Ball feet missing. Late nineteenth-century brown paint over traces of the original green paint. Crest rail, arm supports, legs, and stretchers, maple; spindles, hickory; arms, ash; seat, poplar. SW 23¾″, SD 15¾″, SH 14½″, OH 41″. (Burlington County Historical Society)

Similar to figure 3, this chair has a crest rail with more emphatic curves; ear volutes with more chamfer; less bulbous arm supports with an extra reel before the baluster turning; and a more bulbous medial stretcher with smaller ring turnings. Note the slight concavity in the leg turning, a feature sometimes seen on these chairs. The rolled shape of the seat and the more gently shaped side stretchers indicate a slightly later date for this chair than for figure 3.

5. Armchair. Pennsylvania, possibly Lancaster County; 1750–1770. Original black paint. Crest rail and arms, oak; spindles, hickory; arm supports, legs, and stretchers, maple; seat, pine. SW 24½″, SD 16″, SH 17″, OH 42″. (Tom Brown)

This chair has a Lancaster County ear and medial stretcher, but the chair as a whole is based on a Philadelphia type (compare with figure 3). Note the interesting block turning at the top of the leg before it enters the seat.

4

5

6

7

7.   Armchair. Philadelphia, 1765–1780. Refinished; traces of the original green paint. Crest rail, oak; spindles and arms, hickory; handholds, oak; arm supports, legs, and stretchers, maple; seat, poplar. SW 24¾″, SD 17″, SH 17″, OH 45¼″. (Mr. and Mrs. R. W. P. Allen)

With this chair, we move to a somewhat later, middle-period Philadelphia-style comb-back. The chair has the same generous comb-piece as the earlier chairs, but the turnings have become less distinctive. For example, the legs have a long, rigid baluster and a tapered foot rather than a ball foot. And the baluster-and-ring medial stretcher is later than the Queen Anne stretchers of the earlier chairs.

6.   Armchair. Philadelphia, 1750–1770. Legs pieced out incorrectly; should have ball feet. Early nineteenth-century putty-color paint with black, brown, and green decoration over the original green paint. Crest rail, arms, and handholds, oak; spindles, hickory; arm supports, legs, and stretchers, maple; seat, poplar. SW 24⅝″, SD 16¾″, SH 17¼″, OH 44¾″. (John Bartram Association)

Though it possesses an ample seat, a nicely spread nine-spindle comb, and the same general characteristics as figure 3, this chair does not make as strong a statement. The comb-piece is tamer than that of figure 3, the arm supports not as bulbous, the seat not as deeply saddled.

8. Armchair. New York City, 1765–1780. Nineteenth-century dark brown paint over the original green paint. Crest rail, arm supports, legs, and stretchers, maple; spindles, hickory; arms and handholds, oak; seat, pine. SW 23¾″, SD 17½″, SH 17½ ″, OH 43½″. (James and Nancy Glazer)

At first glance, this chair might be taken for a Philadelphia or Pennsylvania comb-back, but the shape of the crest rail, the arm supports, and especially the leg turnings—with their short baluster and long taper—suggest to me that the chair is one of those rare examples of a New York City comb-back influenced by the Philadelphia style.

9

8

9. Armchair. Philadelphia, 1765–1780. Old refinish. Crest rail, oak; spindles and arm rail, hickory; arm supports, legs, and stretchers, maple; seat, poplar. (Wayne Pratt)

From the seat up, this chair has the general characteristics of comb-backs from the early period. For example, the arm supports are quite similar to those of figure 3, although slimmer. However, the medial stretcher is no longer double-baluster-and-reel turned but has a more generic single bobbin; the side stretchers have been turned symmetrically to accommodate the medial stretcher (i.e., the medial stretcher is not stepped back); and the seat is rounded off at its edges.

10

10.   Armchair. Philadelphia, 1765–1780. Bottoms of handholds missing. Brown varnish over old red paint, over traces of the original green paint. Crest rail and arms, oak; spindles and handholds, hickory; arm supports, legs, and stretchers, maple; seat, poplar. SW 21½″, SD 16¼″, SH 16½″, OH 40¾″. (John Bartram Association)

A comb-back version of the sack-back chairs produced in Philadelphia at that time, this is a well-balanced, well-proportioned example of the later Philadelphia comb-back style. The elliptical seat—a feature of sack-back Windsors—has soft edges and is not as severely carved as the earlier D-shaped seat. The tapered spindles fan outward slightly, and the ears have a relatively small contour with deep carving. Because the arm supports are set back, they can rake forward, and the turning of the bottom of the arm support echoes the concave turning of the leg taper.

The turnings are very vigorous for a Philadelphia chair of this period, and the leg taper is as long, if not longer, than the baluster— just one example of what we mean when we speak of the balance of the turnings.

11

12

12. Armchair. Philadelphia, 1765–1790. Bottoms of knuckles missing. Refinished. Crest rail and arms, oak; spindles, hickory; arm supports, legs, and stretchers, maple. SW 21¼″, SD 16″, SH 17¾″, OH 43¼″. (Mr. and Mrs. R. W. P. Allen)

Here is another example of a middle-period Philadelphia comb-back. Its most unusual feature is its remarkable number of spindles—fifteen in its back, as opposed to the usual nine, and five under each arm where three would be expected.

11. Armchair. Philadelphia, 1765–1780. Bottoms of handholds missing. Very old mahogany varnish over a light ground, over traces of the original green paint. Crest rail, arm supports, legs, and stretchers, maple; spindles and arms, hickory; seat, poplar. SW 21½″, SD 16½″, SH 17″, OH 43″. (Historical Society of Pennsylvania)

This chair is in essentially the same style as figure 10, and its ears are well carved. Yet the chair as a whole is less strong than figure 10. The arm supports are more attenuated. The seat has the same basic elliptical shape but is more vaguely carved. The leg turnings, although typical of the Philadelphia style, are quite slender, and their baluster is longer than their taper, creating the illusion that there is too much distance from the seat to the stretchers.

13

13.   Armchair. Philadelphia, 1765–1790. Branded I. [Joseph] HENZEY. One of a pair. Late eighteenth-century mahoganizing over the original green paint. Crest rail, oak; spindles, hickory; arm crest and seat, poplar; arms and knuckles, mahogany; arm supports, legs, and stretchers, maple. SW 21″, SD 15¾″, SH 17″, OH 42¾″. (Peter Wentz Farmstead)

Though superficially similar to figure 11, this Henzey chair shows certain distinctive structural differences. For one thing, Henzey chose to make the chair with a sawed arm joined by an arm crest—a device not normally associated with Henzey. Furthermore, it is rare to find a Windsor chair of this period that combines a heavy arm crest with an elliptical seat, arm crests usually being found on chairs with shield-shaped seats. It's quite possible that this chair was a special order, made to match a set of other chairs with elliptical seats. Adding weight to this possibility is the fact that the chair has mahogany arms and knuckles, which might also have been specially ordered. (To date I have seen only a few chairs of this type with mahogany arms and knuckles.) The turnings of this chair are better developed than those of figure 11, but they are still not as well balanced as those of figure 10 because, once again, the leg taper is shorter than the second baluster turning.

14. Armchair. Philadelphia, 1765–1780. Medial stretcher and one side stretcher are early replacements. Early nineteenth-century mahoganizing over a salmon-color ground, over the original green paint. Crest rail and arms, oak; spindles, hickory; arm crest and seat, poplar; arm supports, legs, and stretchers, maple. SW 20½″, SD 17″, SH 16½″, OH 42″. (Independence National Historical Park)

Because this chair has a shield-shaped seat, it is more typical of Philadelphia comb-backs of the period with this arm construction. This chair has nine back spindles, although chairs of this type usually have seven spindles in their backs and two short spindles under each arm. The use of the shield-shaped seat not only allows the arm supports to be stepped back quite far but also allows them to have a rakish angle. At the same time, the arms and knuckles appear to have a more dramatic projection than those of most other types of Windsors.

15. Armchair. Philadelphia, 1765–1780. Bottoms of knuckles missing; far right spindle replaced. Black paint over traces of the original green. Crest rail and arms, oak; spindles, hickory; arm supports, legs, and stretchers, maple; seat, poplar. SW 20¼″, SD 16″, SH 16½″, OH 41″. (Independence National Historical Park)

A more typical seven-spindle fan-back with a shield-shaped seat, this chair exhibits a slightly different turning pattern from that of figure 14. Note the thickness of the arm supports as they enter the seat. The leg turnings would be better if they were a bit less rigid.

16

16.   Armchair. Philadelphia, 1765–1780. Early nineteenth-century brownish-red paint over the original green. Crest rail and arms, oak; spindles, hickory; arm crest and seat, poplar; arm supports, legs, and stretchers, maple. SW 19¾", SD 16¾", SH 17¾", OH 41½". (Also see color plate III.) (Privately owned)

This chair is the finest example I have ever seen of a Philadelphia comb-back Windsor with a shield-shaped seat, arm crest, and turned arm supports. It is also the most formal Windsor I have encountered, and I believe it should be considered a masterpiece of its period and of its type. Furthermore, I have seen only one other chair of this type that also has blunt-arrow feet.

So often one can point up excellent details of a particular chair, while other parts can be criticized. Throughout this chair, however, not only are all the individual parts virtually perfect, but they also fit together in perfect harmony. For example, the slightly longer cylinder of the legs supporting a slightly shorter baluster emphasizes the leg splay; and the slightly elongated blunt-arrow feet lift the chair as though on toes. Did the chairmaker intentionally set out to create a perfect Windsor, or did he do it by chance and instinct? I do not know. There is no theory of perfect Windsor chairmaking; there is only the *practice* of chairmaking. And in my experience with hundreds of comb-back armchairs and thousands of Windsors, I have never seen Windsor chairmaking practiced better than in this chair.

16A. Armchair. A side view, showing the dramatic carving of the seat. The angle of the splayed legs emphasizes the rake of the arm supports, and the outward flare of the knuckles reflects the contour of the side of the seat.

17

16A

17. Armchair. Massachusetts, 1770–1800. (Wayne Pratt)
Here is a New England interpretation of what by then had become a very popular Philadelphia style. A heavy arm crest and sawed arms are used, but the two arm pieces are joined in the Rhode Island manner, with a mounted crest. Unlike the knuckles of Philadelphia chairs, these knuckles are carved directly on the ends of the arms, which makes them appear a bit skimpy. This is a pleasing chair with nice splay and balance, but the seat carving and turning patterns are not as dynamic as those of better New England comb-backs. The ears of the comb-piece are smaller than those of comparable Philadelphia chairs, but more exaggerated. Note how the arched, carved contour below the ear is echoed in the carving behind the knuckle.

18. Armchair. Pennsylvania, possibly Philadelphia; 1765–1780. Refinished. Crest rail, legs, and stretchers, maple; spindles, hickory; arm crest and seat, poplar; arms and arm supports, oak. SW 17¼″, SD 16⅛″, SH 15⅜″, OH 39½″. (Privately owned)

A variant of figure 16, this chair has ram's-horn arm supports in the English style. It is a well-proportioned chair with crisp turnings and an interesting medial stretcher. Note the slightly flaring cylinders above the ball feet. The carved ears are beautifully executed but have somewhat longer necks than would ordinarily be found on a Philadelphia product.

19. Armchair. Massachusetts, 1780–1800. Medial stretcher replaced. Refinished. Crest rail and spindles, hickory; arm crest, arms, arm supports, legs, and stretchers, maple; seat, pine. SW 21¼″, SD 15″, SH 17¾″, OH 41″. (Joan and Don Mayoras)

Once again, we see a New England version of a Philadelphia-style comb-back with sawed arms and an arm crest. However, this is a highly stylized chair with a wonderfully flaring comb-piece, nicely carved ears, and spindles with great fanning and taper. Although the knuckles are carved directly on the ends of the arms, and hence are quite thin, they are also rather wide, which compensates for their thinness. The arm supports and legs, though slender, are crisply turned, and the side stretchers are more elaborate than one would expect on such a chair. Note the heavy scoring on the turnings, added as a decorative device. The seat is boldly saddled.

20.   Armchair. Massachusetts, 1780–1800. Very old crackled orange shellac over the original green paint. Crest rail, arm supports, legs, and stretchers, maple; spindles and arms, hickory; seat, pine. SW 21″, SD 15½″, SH 18½″, OH 45½″. (Richard Kozar)

This is a simple but elegant comb-back with crisp, graceful turnings and a well-carved seat. Note that the ears have gouge marks instead of the usual volutes. Over the years I have seen this motif used on several fan-back side chairs, and in every case, the chair's comb-piece has been made of maple. However, I have never seen another comb-back armchair with this motif.

21.   Armchair. New England, probably Massachusetts; 1780–1800. Original black paint. Crest rail and arms, oak; spindles, hickory; arm supports, legs, and stretchers, maple; seat, pine. SW 21″, SD 14¾″, SH 18″, OH 42½″. (Mark and Kathy Winchester)

Almost a study in tapers, this chair has well-defined turnings and a comb-piece with an exceptionally deep bend. All in all, a very dramatic Windsor statement.

20

21

23.   Armchair. Connecticut, 1780–1800. Nineteenth-century black paint with gilt striping over the original gray paint. Crest rail, maple; spindles, hickory; arms, oak; arm supports, legs, and stretchers, maple; seat, pine. SW 20⅛″, SD 14¾″, SH 18″, OH 41″. (Sam Bruccoleri)

The fine comb-piece of this chair—typical of certain Connecticut Windsors—has uncarved, neckless ears that turn upward and have an almost knife-edge thinness at the top. Other typical Connecticut features include the slightly bulbous spindles and the bulbous, high stretchers that narrow before they enter the legs. The heavily chamfered elliptical seat has a sharp pommel. This is a pleasing country product.

22.   Armchair. Rhode Island, 1780–1800. Refinished; traces of dark brown paint. Crest rail, spindles, and arms, hickory; back posts, arm supports, legs, and stretchers, maple; seat, yellow pine. SW 20″, SD 15¼″, OH 38¾″. (Museum of Early Southern Decorative Arts, Winston-Salem, N.C.)

Instead of the conventional tapering spindles, this chair has short, baluster-turned spindles on either end of the comb-piece—a feature occasionally found on Rhode Island Windsors. The effect is the same as that of Rhode Island bow-backs with so-called pipestem spindles (see figure 137). The turning patterns on this chair are typical of Rhode Island.

24. Armchair. Connecticut, probably the Westbrook area; 1780–1800. Nineteenth-century black paint with gilt striping over the original green paint. Crest rail, probably oak; spindles and arms, hickory; arm supports, legs, and stretchers, maple; seat, pine. SW 20½″, SD 15″, SH 18⅛″, OH 40″. (Kathleen Mulhern)

This is a more successful chair than figure 23 in practically every way except for the seat carving and the medial stretcher. The turning pattern is influenced by New York City Windsors.

24

25

25. Armchair. Connecticut, 1780–1800. Painted red. Crest rail and arms, ash; spindles, hickory; arm supports, legs, and stretchers, maple; seat, pine. SW 16¾″, SD 17½″, SH 17″, OH 37¾″. (Joan and Don Mayoras)

Judging by the large number of Connecticut comb-backs in this style that have been discovered, this type of chair must have been nearly as popular in Connecticut as the sack-back was in Philadelphia. Characteristically on the small side, these chairs usually have narrow ears that flare up; bulbous, tapering spindles; an arm rail with tiny handholds that echo the shape of the ears; and a shield-shaped seat. On this example, the seat seems a bit too thick for the small size of the chair. The baluster turnings are nicely done and seem to be influenced by New York City Windsors.

26. Armchair. Hudson River Valley or southern Connecticut, 1780–1800. Painted olive green. SW 21″, SD 15½″, SH 15¼″, OH 39″. (The Robert Wagner Collection)

This is an extremely interesting chair with arm-support and leg turnings like ones I have seen in other Windsors from the Hudson River Valley area. Possibly there is a Dutch influence at work here, since at least one other chair with similar turnings is branded HERRCK (see figure 91). Another similarity to figure 91 is the seat carving. Figure 94, a Connecticut sack-back, also has a similar seat carving. Note the pinwheel design on the ears and handholds—a favorite Connecticut motif. The piercing of the comb-piece is an unusual design feature. The comb-piece is basically Connecticut in style because of its upturned ears, reflecting the strong English influence on many Connecticut Windsor crest rails.

27. Armchair. Pennsylvania, 1790–1810. Seat upholstery is a later addition to cover potty cutout. Painted pale green, with arm supports painted orange, over the original dark green. Crest rail, arms, and legs, oak; spindles, hickory; arm supports and stretchers, maple; seat, pine. SW 20″, SD 15½″, SH 18½″, OH 44½″. (Eugene Pettinelli)

The legs and medial stretcher of this chair have bamboo-turned double bobbins, but the side stretchers and arm supports are baluster-turned. The bamboo leg turnings are typical of Pennsylvania. The chair is sturdy and well proportioned for such a late Windsor.

26

27

LOW-BACK

~

CHAIRS

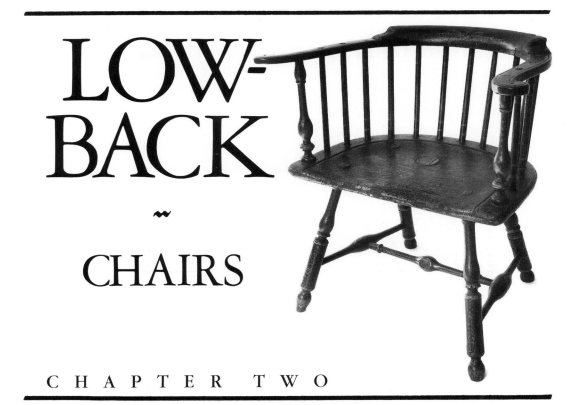

Like comb-back Windsors, low-backs are mainly identified with Philadelphia. When they were produced in other areas—as they seldom were—they were usually heavily influenced by the Philadelphia product.

Most of the Philadelphia examples display such early characteristics as untapered spindles, D-shaped seats, scrolled handholds, Queen Anne medial stretchers, and cylinder-and-ball feet. The only low-back form that stands apart is the Newport, Rhode Island, low-back, with its cross-stretchers and basically English design. (Those chairs, by the way, are often made of a single wood, such as maple or chestnut.)

By the 1770s, only a small proportion of Philadelphia low-back Windsor chairs reflected the latest fashion in Windsor design.[1] However, it is interesting to note that while few Windsor low-back chairs were produced during the bamboo period in Philadelphia (1785–1800), many Philadelphia low-back settees with bamboo turnings were made.

The low-back continued to be produced in smaller and smaller quantities during the first years of the nineteenth century. But the form was never part of the mainstream of Windsor fashion, and was always to remain a mid-eighteenth-century style.

28. Armchair. Philadelphia, 1740–1760. Nineteenth-century black paint over red, over the original green. Arm crest, arm supports, legs, and stretchers, maple; spindles, hickory; arms, oak; seat, poplar. SW 24¾″; SD 17⅛″; SH 17″; OH 28½″. (David Miller)

This is a classic Philadelphia low-back Windsor of the early period. The double-baluster-and-reel medial stretcher—sometimes called a Queen Anne stretcher—is socketed into the side stretchers with abrupt ball turnings. Here we also see the classic Philadelphia leg, with the top baluster buried midway into the underside of the seat; the elongated baluster turnings below that, over a reel and ring; and then a cylinder and the characteristic Philadelphia ball foot.

Note especially the turning pattern of the arm supports. There is a baluster turning right below the arm rail—very characteristic of the early chairs—which is turnip-like. It sits on a flaring collar, followed by a narrow cylinder, then an abrupt baluster, a thin neck, a wide ring, a thin neck, and, finally, a ring made to look like a ball buried deep in the seat.

The seat is characteristically D-shaped, with sharp, angular chamfering. The spindles are vertical, with no taper.

29. Armchair. Philadelphia, 1750–1770. Medial stretcher probably an early replacement; end piece of arm crest missing on right side. Nineteenth-century red paint over the original green. Arm crest and seat, poplar; spindles, hickory; arms, oak; arm supports, legs, and stretchers, maple. SW 25″, SD 17⅛″, SH 16¼″, OH 27½″. (Philip Bradley Antiques)

Although this low-back has many of the characteristics of figure 28, it is probably somewhat later because the turning pattern has been toned down, which is especially evident in the side stretchers. The paint surface and overall condition are good for such an early chair.

28

29

30.   Armchair. Philadelphia, 1765–1780. Branded R-B. One of a pair. Late nineteenth-century black paint, over red, over the original green. Arm crest and seat, poplar; spindles, hickory; arms, white oak; arm supports, legs, and stretchers, maple. SW 24⅝″, SD 17⅜″, SH 16¼″, OH 28¾″. (Independence National Historical Park)

Here is a good example of a slightly later version of the Philadelphia low-back. We can see the turnings beginning to change: the balusters have become much more gentle in their flow; the turnip-like turning at the top of the arm support has become smaller and not as bulbous; the collar above the reel at midleg has a rounded shoulder and is not as high and crisp. Note that the medial stretcher has a bulbous baluster turning with a ring on either side. The side stretchers, although similar to those of figure 29, no longer have the abrupt center ball turnings of figure 28.

The R-B brand is probably the identification mark of an owner. The chair has a New York State history, and owners' brands seem to have been common there.

31

30

31.   Armchair. Philadelphia area, 1765–1780. Refinished. Arm crest, poplar; spindles, ash; arms, oak; arm supports, legs, and stretchers, maple; seat, pine. SW 23⅞″, SD 17″, SH 17¼″, OH 29″. (Burlington County Historical Society)

The feet, legs and spindles of this chair offer additional evidence of how turning styles change over time. First, this chair has blunt-arrow feet, as opposed to ball feet. The balusters and medial stretcher are like those found on chairs in such outlying areas of Philadelphia as Bucks and Chester counties. Note also the slight taper of the spindles, an indication of lateness on these chairs. In this photograph, the decorative score marks on the tops of the arms can be seen clearly.

32. Armchair. Philadelphia, 1765–1780. Marked A.C.J. PAINTER 1888 on the seat bottom. Medial stretcher bobbin broken in the center. Late-nineteenth-century grain-painted to imitate rosewood, over a salmon-color ground, over the original green paint with yellow decoration. Arm crest and seat, poplar; spindles, hickory; arms, oak; arm supports, legs, and stretchers, maple. SW 24¾″, SD 16¾″, SH 17″, OH 28¾″. (Claude and Alvan Bisnoff)

Note the slight concavity of the leg cylinders, a feature of some Philadelphia low-backs and comb-backs. The side stretchers are unusually bulbous for this sort of chair. In addition to being a fine example of its type, this chair is also interesting for its late nineteenth-century paint decoration, used to update a Windsor form that had come back into fashion as a so-called captain's chair.

33. Armchair. Philadelphia area, 1765–1790. Old refinish. Arm crest, poplar; spindles, hickory; arms, chestnut; arm supports, legs, and stretchers, maple; seat, pine. SW 23¾″, SD 16″, SH 15¾″, OH 27½″. (Burlington County Historical Society)

A provincial copy of a Philadelphia form, this chair is not as sophisticated as previous examples. Thick throughout, the arm rail and arm supports seem a bit clumsy. The leg turnings are not well proportioned, and the cylinders are too wide and too long for the size of the balusters. The abrupt bulb in the medial stretcher makes the ends of the stretcher seem sticklike.

32

33

34

34.   Armchair. Philadelphia, 1765–1780. Refinished; traces of white paint over the original green. Arm crest and seat, poplar; spindles, hickory; arms and arm supports, oak; legs and stretchers, maple. SW 18⅜″, SD 17″, SH 17¾″, OH 29⅜″. (Eugene Pettinelli)

The fact that this is a Philadelphia low-back in the English or High Wickham style, as opposed to a comb-back, makes this an extremely rare form—and indeed, it is the only such chair I have seen. Nevertheless, there is no doubt that this chair was originally made as a low-back and is not simply a comb-back that has lost its comb. First, the spindles do not penetrate the arm crest; second, the arm crest itself rolls over in the back, as it would not do on a comb-back.

Its English features include the ram's-horn arm supports and the shovel-shaped seat, which is squared off on the back edge and which has no "rain gutter."[2] The chamfering on either side of each scrolled arm is unusual, but the blunt-arrow feet and the stretchers are typical Philadelphia products.

35. Armchair. Newport, Rhode Island, 1764. Made for Newport's Redwood Library and Atheneum in 1764, probably by Timothy Waterhouse. One of 12. Black paint over several other coats of paint, over the original bottle green. Made entirely in maple, except the pine seat. SW 22″, SD 15⅛″, SH 16″, OH 27½″. (The Redwood Library and Atheneum)

Based on physical evidence of the Windsors I have seen over the years, I am increasingly convinced that very few Windsor chairs were produced in New England prior to the end of the Revolutionary War. Before that time, New England residents were saturated, and apparently satisfied, with the exported products of Philadelphia Windsor makers. However, in Newport, Rhode Island—a center of high-style furniture—the type of low-back Windsor shown here was produced almost in isolation before 1776. The Redwood Library and Atheneum has documentation indicating that this particular chair—part of a set of 12—was purchased in 1764.

As far as we know, this is the earliest type of Windsor produced in New England, and it shows a strong English influence in the turning patterns of its arm supports and legs. The back construction and cross-stretchers are quite similar to those of formal Newport cabriole-leg corner chairs of the period. Note especially the small arrows at the ends of the stretchers just before they enter the legs. Also shown clearly in the photo is the back construction: the arm crest sits atop the sawed arms, which meet in the back of the chair in a butt joint. (In Philadelphia low-backs, the arm crest is attached with a lap joint.) Similar Rhode Island Windsors exist, but they are provincial-looking and were probably not made in Newport. This is another example of how Windsor chairmakers interpreted more formal designs of the period.

35

36.   Armchair. Pennsylvania, 1765–1790. Refinished; traces of white paint and the original green paint. Arms, arm supports, seat, legs, and stretchers, poplar; spindles, ash. SW 20⅝″, SD 16⅝″, SH 18″, OH 28¼″. (Corinne and Chris Machmer)

This is the only low-back Windsor of its type that I have ever seen. However, while it may be unique, it is related to a group of three low-back settees in the same style, two of which are shown in figures 208 and 209 and which were found in the Pennsylvania-Maryland border area. The leg turning and stretchers of this piece are identical to those of figure 209. Unlike most low-backs, this chair does not have a separate arm crest; instead, the arms with their false crest are made in two pieces that are joined in the back with a large dovetail joint.

The elliptical seat, with its pronounced pommel and heavy chamfering, as well as the stretcher turnings, are like those found on Lancaster County, Pennsylvania, fan-backs and sack-backs. Also, the seat is quite thick (about three inches), another provincial characteristic. Although the spindles are not decoratively turned, as they are on figures 208 and 209, they do angle progressively outward from the center until the outermost spindles match the angle of the arm supports. Overall, this is a very fine and interesting chair that, unfortunately, has been refinished.

37.   Armchair. Probably New Jersey; early nineteenth century. Crackled dark brown varnish, probably original. Arm crest, probably maple; spindles, hickory; arms, oak; arm supports, legs, and stretchers, maple; seat, poplar or pine. SW 25″, SD 16″, SH 16⅞″, OH 27″. (Privately owned; courtesy of Federation Antiques, Inc.)

I have seen several comb-backs with turnings similar to those of this chair that have come from the Trenton, New Jersey, area. They were probably produced in the same shop during the first quarter of the nineteenth century. The legs are reminiscent of the work of a spinning-wheel maker.

37

36

FAN-BACK

~

CHAIRS

Fan-back side chairs were produced in large numbers, not only in Philadelphia but also in New England. The armchair variety seems to have been most popular in coastal Massachusetts, including Nantucket—whose craftsmen were probably influenced by the small quantity of Philadelphia fan-back armchairs produced and exported. In Philadelphia, the fan-back armchair was made in both the blunt-arrow and later tapered-leg style, whereas in coastal Massachusetts the tapered-leg style dominated.

Oddly enough, the fan-back chair seems to have been largely ignored by the New York City chairmakers. Over the years I have seen only a handful that might have been produced in New York, and none that I would judge to be unequivocally New York in origin.

Like the Massachusetts fan-backs, those from Rhode Island often display a Philadelphia influence. Perhaps half of the Connecticut fan-backs use a comb-piece with uncarved, turned-up ears reminiscent of English, rather than Philadelphia, models. The bulk of the Connecticut, the Rhode Island, and the Massachusetts fan-backs have ears that turn down and have carved volutes. Generally speaking, when carved volutes are used, the ear contour turns down; when the ears are plain, the contour turns up. The plain, upturned comb-piece does show up in the simpler Philadelphia versions. In New England, this plain comb-piece often appears in certain otherwise quite elaborate fan-backs, especially those from Connecticut.

38.   Armchair. New England, probably Newport, Rhode Island; 1765–1780. Original greenish-black paint with gilt striping and decoration. Crest rail and arms, oak; back posts and spindles, hickory; seat, pine; arm supports, legs, and stretchers, maple. SW 19¾″, SD (including tailpiece) 20½″, SH 17″, OH 41½″. (Bernard & S. Dean Levy, Inc.)

An elegant example of a New England fan-back armchair, this type was first produced in Philadelphia and modeled after English chairs.[3] Particularly fine features include the arm scroll, reminiscent of Philadelphia low-back Windsor handholds, and the beautifully turned blunt-arrow feet, which retain their full height. Interestingly, in the English fashion, the legs of this chair do not penetrate the seat, which is practically full-round with the wood grain running on the diagonal so that the tailpiece can be cut directly from the seat plank. In Philadelphia, this type of chair always seems to be a brace-back. Other typical Philadelphia characteristics include five long, almost perpendicular spindles; back posts that fan out; and bracing spindles filling the space between the back posts and back spindles.

38

39

39.   Armchair. Philadelphia, 1765–1780. Early nineteenth-century black paint over the original olive green. Crest rail, back posts, arm supports, legs, and stretchers, maple; spindles, maple or hickory; arms, oak; seat, poplar. SW 19″, SD 17″, tailpiece 3⅞″, SH 17″. (Chester County Historical Society)

Although this fan-back armchair is generally constructed like the one in figure 38, an obvious difference is the crest rail, which is similar to the arm crest of a low-back Windsor. The back posts have a long baluster above the arm, and the scrolled arms end abruptly and look like unfinished knuckle handholds—a not uncommon feature of these chairs. The medial stretcher has no rings, and the legs do penetrate the seat.

40.   Armchair. New York, 1770–1790. Nineteenth-century black paint with yellow striping and decoration over the original green. Crest rail, oak; spindles and back posts, hickory; arms, arm supports, legs, and stretchers, maple; seat, poplar. SW 18¾", SD (including tailpiece) 19¾", SH 17¼", OH 43½". (Suzanne Courcier and Robert Wilkins)

The basic style of this chair is that of Philadelphia. Similarities include the ringed back posts, the flaring, scrolled ears, and abruptly ending arms. But the leg turnings are quite different, and typical of New York City in their bulbousness and long taper. The seat, though round, has not been carved well from underneath to create the illusion of thinness, suggesting that the chair may be provincial and not from New York City. Similarly, the arms have a provincial thickness. Such chairs were produced mainly in Philadelphia and Massachusetts, and it is rare to find one with New York turnings.

41.   Armchair. Pennsylvania, 1770–1790. Very old black paint with gilt striping over the original black. Crest rail, oak; spindles, hickory; arms, arm supports, legs, and stretchers, maple; seat, pine. SW 18", SD 16", SH 16", OH 40". (Tom Brown)

Over the years this type of chair has come to be called a "lady's chair" because of its narrowness. It is an unusual form, and probably a provincial example of a much more sophisticated Philadelphia type. The chair has the blunt-arrow feet of the earlier 1750–1770 period, but the tops of the legs and the arm supports are in a later style. The seat is nicely sculpted but a litte too thick, making the undercarriage appear too small. The necks of the ears are long and rather quaint, and, interestingly, the volutes are only painted on, not carved. The center back spindle has been turned to echo the shape of the arm supports. Every time I have seen a similar center spindle on a fan-back Windsor, the chair has not been a brace-back; it is as though the added "back post" gives the chair enough extra strength to make back bracing unnecessary.

42. Side chair. Philadelphia, 1780–1800. Branded J[ohn] STOW PHIL.[A] *fecit*. Refinished. Crest rail, oak; spindles and back post, hickory; seat, poplar; legs and stretchers, maple. (Independence National Historical Park)

This is a "garden variety" nine-spindle fan-back of its period, but it is interesting because it is the only known chair branded by John Stow. Furthermore, it is very unusual to find a Philadelphia product with the words *fecit Phila.,* or "made in Philadelphia," branded in Latin or in any other language.

43. Side chair. Philadelphia, 1765–1780. Branded I. [Joseph] HENZEY. Very old black paint over the original green. Crest rail, oak; spindles and back posts, hickory; seat, poplar; legs and stretchers, maple. SW 18½″, SD 17″, SH 18″, OH 38″. (Privately owned)

In comparison with figure 42, this is a very ambitious chair in the highest style. It has crisp turnings, beautifully scrolled ears, and a broad, well-saddled seat.

42

43

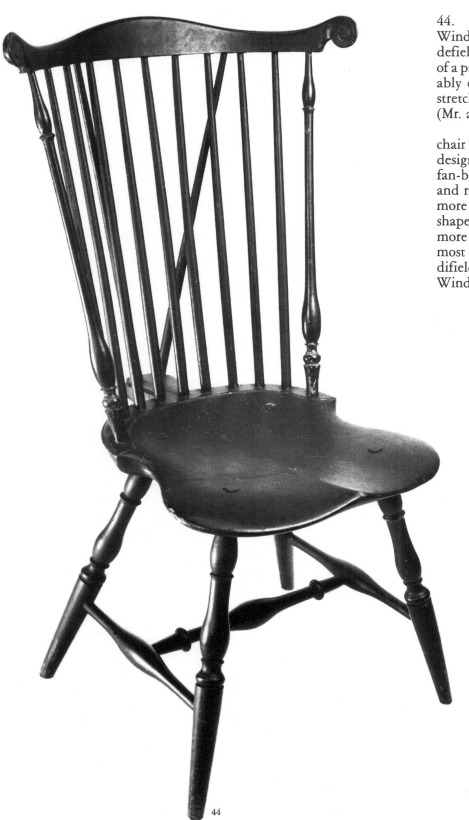

44.   Side chair. Philadelphia, 1765–1790. Label reads: "Maker of Windsor and rush bottom chairs/Made and sold by/William Widdefield [sic]/in Spruce St. below the drawbridge/Philadelphia." One of a pair. Very old black paint over the original green. Crest rail, probably oak; spindles and back posts, hickory; seat, poplar; legs and stretchers, maple. SW 17½", SD 17", tailpiece 4", SH 18", OH 39¼". (Mr. and Mrs. Victor Johnson)

Far more elegant than the typical Philadelphia product, this chair betters even the one in figure 43. Here we see all of the brilliant design and proportions of the best Connecticut and Massachusetts fan-backs. The long taper of the legs, for example, is quite graceful and rarely found on Philadelphia Windsors. The back is taller and more narrow-waisted than those of most Philadelphia chairs, the shape of the comb-piece has a more distinctive roll, and the seat is more deeply saddled. Furthermore, this is a brace-back chair, and most Philadelphia fan-backs were not made this way. Perhaps Widdifield, known to be a Philadelphian, had studied New England Windsors and was influenced by their designs.

44

45.   Side chair. Philadelphia, 1780–1800. Branded L[awrence] ALLWINE. Reupholstered. Nineteenth-century black paint, over the original moss green, over a red ground. Crest rail and back posts, oak; spindles, hickory; seat, poplar; legs and stretchers, maple. SW 18″, SD 15½″, SH 18½″, OH 36½″. (James Brooks)

Because the seat of this chair was carved to be fitted with upholstery, it is not saddled. On the front of the comb-piece, spindles, legs, and stretchers is ornamental gouge carving, which was probably executed in the early nineteenth century to update the chair and make it fit in with the then fashionable "fancy" chairs.

46.   Side chair. Pennsylvania, possibly Philadelphia; 1770–1790. Original dark mustard-color paint, oxidized to a dark brown. Crest rail, oak; back posts, ash; spindles, hickory; seat, poplar; legs and stretchers, maple. SW 17⅜″, SD 15½″, tailpiece 2″, SH 18″, OH 36½″. (Nancy and Tom Tafuri)

This chair is something of a puzzle. The seat and leg turnings are finely executed and have a Philadelphia look, but the medial stretcher and the comb-piece seem provincial. Also, Philadelphia chairs of this type usually have shorter backs and uncarved ears. Thus it is difficult to pinpoint the origin of this piece. The original paint has oxidized nicely to a deep brown.

48.   Side chair. Richmond, Virginia, 1780–1800. Label reads: "Made and Warranted by William Pointer." Refinished. Crest rail, legs, and stretchers, maple; back posts, ash; spindles, hickory; seat, poplar. SW 16⅞", SD 16", SH 16⁹⁄₁₆", OH 35⅜". (Museum of Early Southern Decorative Arts, Winston-Salem, N.C.)

William Pointer was a Virginia chairmaker who was apparently influenced by Windsors made in Philadelphia. This is a pleasing chair, but it does not have the authority of the Philadelphia product.

47.   Side chair. Philadelphia, 1770–1790. Nineteenth-century reddish-brown paint over traces of the original green. Crest rail, oak; back posts and spindles, hickory; seat, poplar; legs and stretchers, maple. SW 17¾", SD 16¼", SH 18", OH 35¾". (Eugene Pettinelli)

A very well-proportioned fan-back, this is the type of chair that was exported by the thousands from Philadelphia by Stephen Girard and other shippers and chairmakers.

49. Side chair. Chester County, Pennsylvania, 1780–1800. Branded J[esse] CUSTER. Late nineteenth-century black paint over the original green. Crest rail, oak; back posts, legs, and stretchers, maple; spindles, hickory; seat, poplar. SW 17¼″, SD 16⅛″, SH 17″, OH 37″. (Lori and Craig Mayor)

Because of the slender taper of its legs, which Custer seems to have used in most of his leg turnings, this is a very elegant side chair—more graceful than most Pennsylvania side chairs. The chair would be even better if it had carved ears.

49

50

50. Side chair. Lancaster County, Pennsylvania, 1760–1780. Early nineteenth-century dark red crackled varnish. Crest rail, back posts, and spindles, hickory; seat, poplar; legs and stretchers, maple. SW 19¼″, SD 15¼″, SH 17″, OH 37″. (Privately owned)

Here is certainly one of the most beautiful examples of this type of Lancaster County Windsor. The comb-piece is of the finest design that can be found in Lancaster County. And note the blunt-arrow feet: they are wider in diameter than the rest of the legs. This means that the maker turned the legs narrower than the feet, chiseling away the extra wood—an extremely unusual technique for a Windsor chair. This technique requires extra work and is much like the method used in making certain early Pennsylvania slat-back chairs which have ball feet that are wider than the rest of the legs.

51

51.   Side chair. Lancaster County, Pennsylvania, 1780–1800. Reddish-brown paint with blue striping over the original green paint. Crest rail and spindles, hickory or ash; back posts, ash; seat, poplar; legs and stretchers, maple. SW 19″, SD 15″, SH 16½″, OH 37½″. (Marjorie Hooper)

This is another superb example of Lancaster County Windsor-making with the same Germanic feeling as figure 50. In fact, the design seems akin to certain Moravian chairs with stick legs and plank seats. The ears are higher than those of figure 50, the comb-piece is wider, and the back posts are more elaborately turned. On the other hand, the slimmer turnings of figure 50 make the seat look taller and the chair as a whole more stately. It's a toss-up as to which chair is better. Note how the back of figure 51 does not seem to fan out but simply leans backward; this is a common feature of many Lancaster County fan-backs.

52.   Side chair. Lancaster County, Pennsylvania, 1770–1790. Traces of original green paint. Crest rail, back posts, and spindles, hickory; seat, poplar; legs and stretchers, maple. SW 16¾″, SD 15½″, SH 14″, OH 34″. (Frank Rentschler)

Note the modified blunt-arrow leg design on this chair. The cylinder has been shortened above the foot to achieve a low overall height for the chair. With this type of leg—as opposed to the tapered leg—the maker had to custom-reproportion the length of the cylinder to make the chair higher or lower; with the tapered leg, all he had to do was cut the leg to the desired length. Short chairs like this are often called "slipper chairs." This one has all the characteristic Lancaster County features except an imposing comb-piece.

52

53.   Side chair. Probably Lancaster County, Pennsylvania; 1775–
1790. Refinished. Crest rail, back posts, and spindles, hickory; seat,
poplar; legs and stretchers, maple. SW 19″, SD 14¾″, SH 17″, OH
36″. (Robert Stallfort)
    This is a very simplified chair with generic back posts and legs
in the Philadelphia style. The seat shape, however, is typical of Lancaster County. Note the similarity to the crest rail of figure 52.

54.   Side chair. Connecticut, 1790–1810. Branded S. McCOR-
MICK. Nineteenth-century beige paint over red, over black, over the
original green. Crest rail, hickory; back posts, legs, and stretchers,
pine; spindles, ash; seat, poplar. SW 15⅝″, SD 16¼″, tailpiece 2⅜″,
SH 16¼″, OH 35⁵⁄₁₆″ (Steven and Helen Kellogg)
    It is very unusual for the turned parts of a Windsor chair to be
made of pine, as they are in this chair. Because pine is relatively soft,
the legs, stretchers, and back posts are not turned as crisply as they
might have been. Overall, the chair has a country look.

55. Side chair. Connecticut, 1790–1810. Early nineteenth-century black paint, ringed and striped with gilt, over the original green paint. Crest rail, ash; back posts, hickory or ash; spindles, hickory; seat, pine; legs and stretchers, maple. SW 15″, SD 15½″, SH 15¼″, OH 35¼″. (Melissa and Gary Lipton)

The sides of the seats of Connecticut chairs are usually heavily chamfered, as here. The back posts have an interesting long taper, and the legs are unusual because there is no turning on them before they enter the seat. Note the decorative leaf carving on the ears—another unusual feature.

56. Side chair. Probably New York City; 1780–1800. Refinished; weathered surface. Crest rail, oak; back posts, chestnut; spindles, hickory; seat, pine; legs and stretchers, maple. SW 17″, SD 16⅛″, SH 16¾″, OH 37″. (Philip Bradley Antiques)

Sack-backs, bow-backs, and continuous-arm chairs from New York City are quite common, but fan-backs are almost nonexistent. Nevertheless, this chair may be one of those rarities. The thicks and thins of the turnings are remarkably like those of other known New York City Windsors. Note the beautifully carved ears with very short necks. If the chair is from New York City, it may explain why the necks are so short in comparison with similar chairs from nearby areas such as Connecticut.

55

56

57

58

58.   Side chair. Connecticut, possibly the Westbrook area; 1780–1800. Early nineteenth-century dark red paint striped with gilt over the original blackish-green paint; seat has a coat of black varnish. Crest rail, oak; back posts, legs, and stretchers, maple; spindles, ash; seat, pine. SW 15½″, SD 17¾″, SH 17½″, OH 36⅞″. (Nancy and Tom Tafuri)

This is a very vigorously turned fan-back typical of Windsors from the Westbrook area of Connecticut. Note the nicely sculpted seat and the high taper of the back posts.

57.   Armchair. Probably Connecticut; 1780–1800. Early blue-green paint over original salmon ground. Crest rail and spindles, hickory; back posts, arms, arm supports, legs, and side stretchers, maple; seat, pine; medial stretcher, chestnut. SW 23½″, SD 16″, SH 18″, OH 48½″. (Privately owned; courtesy of James and Nancy Glazer)

An exceptionally tall chair with an almost fully vertical stance, this is a good example of a tenon-arm fan-back without bracing spindles. The crest rail is beautifully scrolled, like that of figure 56, and the spindles show a kind of Connecticut swelling. The back posts are modestly turned, with the most complex parts right below the crest rail. The legs and stretchers are typical of the type found on many Connecticut Windsor fan-backs. However, it is unusual to find a Connecticut Windsor with a D-shaped seat—a seat shape that almost dictates vertical arm supports with no rake.

59.   Side chair. Connecticut, 1790–1810. Nineteenth-century varnish over the original green paint with gilt striping. Crest rail, back posts, and spindles, hickory; seat, pine; legs and stretchers, maple. SW 14⅛″, SD 15¾″, SH 16½″, OH 36½″. (Nancy and Tom Tafuri)

Connecticut seems to have produced endless examples of very good, stylized provincial chairs, of which this is one. The crest rail rolls in almost to the first spindle, and the seat is heavily chamfered. Note the double baluster-and-reel medial stretcher, which is also found on Connecticut furniture made in styles other than Windsor.

59

60.   Side chair. Connecticut, 1780–1810. Nineteenth-century black paint striped with gilt over earlier red paint. Crest rail and spindles, hickory; back posts, legs, and stretchers, maple; seat, pine. SW 14¼″, SD 17″, SH 14¼″, OH 34¼″. (Privately owned)

This relatively small "youth" chair is, in the Connecticut tradition, highly idiosyncratic. The crest rail is V-notched, and the contour of the seat on the front edge is nearly round. The turning pattern of the medial stretcher can also be found on certain Connecticut rush-bottom chairs.

61. Side chair. Connecticut, Roxbury area, 1780–1810. Nineteenth-century black paint over the original salmon red. Crest rail, back posts, and stretchers, chestnut; spindles, hickory; seat, pine. SW 17¼″, SD 16″, SH 17″, OH 36½″. (Also see color plate XIV.) (Charles Sterling)

Here is another charming, zany example of the imagination of Connecticut Windsor chairmakers. Note the crest rail with its pinwheel carving—a motif found on all sorts of Connecticut furniture. The seat, with its cleft front, is an exaggerated form of the traditional shield-shaped seat. By comparison with the rest of the chair, the legs and stretchers seem rather tame, but such inconsistencies are normal on provincial Windsors.

61

62. Side chair. Connecticut, 1780–1810. Original black paint over a gray ground. Crest rail, back posts, spindles, and stretchers, hickory; seat, pine; legs, maple. SW 17″, SD 14½″, tailpiece 3¾″, SH 16″, OH 37¼″. (Bernard & S. Dean Levy, Inc.)

The cupid's-bow crest rail is a wonderfully idiosyncratic conceit, and very "Connecticut." The terminations of the ears are reminiscent of so-called statehouse Windsors from the Hartford area. The bulbous spindles and the arrows at the ends of the stretchers are also Connecticut features, but the turning pattern is quite individualistic, as is the rotated H-stretcher arrangement. Note that the tailpiece is part of a spline that runs from the front to the back of the seat; the front edge of the spline can be seen in the photograph.

63

63.   Armchair. Coastal Massachusetts, possibly Nantucket; 1780–1800. Mid-nineteenth-century red paint over the original green paint with salmon striping. Crest rail, oak; back posts, arm supports, legs, and stretchers, maple; spindles, hickory; arms, birch; seat, pine. SW 21⅞″, SD 16¼″, tailpiece 4⅜″, SH 15¾″, OH 41¾″. (Steven and Helen Kellogg)

This type of tenoned knuckle-arm Windsor always seems to emphasize the design of the back and arms over the design of the undercarriage. The back of this particular chair is the finest of its type, and the back posts are extraordinary. So often in these chairs all the decorative turnings of the back posts occur above the arms, but on this chair the back posts are also turned below the arms. The crest rail, with its small scrolled ears and long necks, is very well designed. The tailpiece is a separate piece of wood that is mortised into the seat, as is usual in chairs of this type.

64.   Armchair. Coastal Massachusetts, 1780–1800. Old shellac
finish over traces of yellow paint, over a gray ground. Crest rail, oak;
back posts and spindles, hickory; arms, arm supports, legs, and
stretchers, maple; seat, pine. SW 22⅜″, SD 17⅞″, SH 17½″, OH
43¾″. (Mr. and Mrs. R. W. P. Allen)

Fan-back armchairs, although relatively rare, seem to turn up
in the coastal Massachusetts area more often than anywhere else,
including Philadelphia. They usually have certain characteristics—
with, of course, variations in detail. As in this case, the seats are elliptical and the tailpiece is usually a mortised-on addition. This chair has
very sensuous arms and knuckles. The elaborately saddled seat has a
great overhang in relation to the legs. This is a particularly handsome
chair, albeit a bit more conservative than the one shown in figure 63.
Here, the back posts seem to keep themselves much more in place as
back posts, complementing rather than upstaging the leg turnings.
The medial stretcher with its waferlike rings is characteristic of this
Windsor. Note the simplified ear volutes compared with Philadelphia examples (see figure 44).

64

65. Side chair. Massachusetts, 1780–1800. Nineteenth-century black paint striped with gilt over the original gray-green paint. Crest rail, hickory or oak; back posts, legs, and stretchers, maple; spindles, hickory; seat, pine. SW 17″, SD 16½″, SH 18″, OH 37½″. (Sam Bruccoleri)

    The leg turnings of this beautiful Massachusetts fan-back are perfectly balanced, and the vigorous turnings of the back posts, which can sometimes be spindly on these chairs, are in this case a match for the legs. The crest rail is quite nice, with a fine flourish to the ears.

66. Side chair. Massachusetts, 1780–1800. Traces of old black paint over traces of the original green. Crest rail, back posts, legs, and stretchers, chestnut; spindles, hickory; seat, pine. SW 17¼″, SD 16½″, SH 17¾″. (John Bartram Association)

    Compared with figure 65, this chair seems delicate. Yet the crest rails and the seats of the two are almost identical.

67.   Side chair. Massachusetts, 1780–1800. Very old tobacco-brown shellac over traces of yellow paint, over traces of the original green paint. Crest rail, ash; back posts, legs, and stretchers, maple; spindles, hickory; seat, pine. SW 17¾″, SD 17″, SH 17½″, OH 35″. (Privately owned)

      The crest rail of this beautifully turned and well-proportioned chair does not terminate in the usual turned volutes but in rosettes—a popular motif more common to bonnet-top highboys and other case pieces from Massachusetts, Connecticut, and Rhode Island. The seat is a very thick 2¾ inches.

67A.   Side chair. Detail of rosette terminating crest rail.

67

67A

68. Side chair. Boston or possibly Rhode Island; 1780–1810. Old varnish over the original gray paint. Crest rail, legs, and stretchers, maple; back posts and seat, chestnut; spindles, hickory. SW 16⅛″, SD 16″, SH 17¼″, OH 34″. (Philip Bradley Antiques)

Very stylized, this chair has fine leg splay and a well-carved seat. The seat is almost flat on the bottom and is carved on the top. The legs are Rhode Island in style. The crest rail is not as well realized as the rest of the chair. The back posts are idiosyncratic, and there are six back spindles instead of the more common seven.

68

69

69. Side chair. Rhode Island, 1780–1800. Branded U. TUFTS. Old green paint over lighter green. Back posts, legs, and stretchers, maple; spindles, ash; seat, walnut. (David A. Schorsch, Inc.)

This is quite simply one of the finest Rhode Island fan-backs, with extraordinarily bold, crisp turnings.

71.   Side chair. Probably the Boston area; 1790–1810. One of four. Old blackish-green paint over the original brown; seat, buff color. Crest rail and spindles, hickory; back posts and legs, maple; seat, pine; stretchers, chestnut. SW 14¾″, SD 15½″, SH 17¼″, OH 36″. (Privately owned)

This is a small chair with a small seat. The thick bamboo spindles, which are almost as heavy as the back posts, are typical of chairs known to be from the Boston area, and their design compensates for the ordinariness of the undercarriage.

70.   Side chair. Connecticut, 1780–1800. Nineteenth-century black paint with gilt striping over older white paint, over the original green. Crest rail, oak; back posts and spindles, hickory; seat, pine; legs, maple; stretchers, chestnut. SW 15″, SD 16¾″, SH 14½″, OH 35″. (Mr. and Mrs. Paul Flack)

For a chair of such small overall size, this chair has a high back. It was probably intended as a youth chair. Note the finely shaped spindles and boldly turned legs.

72. Side chair. Connecticut, 1790–1810. Original black paint with late-nineteenth-century decoration. Crest rail, back posts, spindles, legs, and stretchers, hickory; seat, chestnut. SW 16¾″, SD 15⅞″, SH 18″, OH 36³⁄₁₆″. (Steven and Helen Kellogg)

The combination of bamboo legs and medial stretcher with baluster side stretchers and back posts turned in the Connecticut pattern is interesting. The crest rail is quite simple, but nicely realized.

73. Side chair. Maine, 1790–1820. Original black paint with gilt and red decoration. Crest rail, ash; back posts and spindles, hickory or ash; seat, pine; legs and stretchers, maple. SW 13¾″, SD 15½″, SH 18″, OH 33⅞″. (Janie and Dr. Peter Gross)

Because the ears of its crest rail do not project upward, the overall feeling of this graceful chair is like that of a rod-back Windsor. The beautifully designed bamboo legs, with turnings balanced like those of the earlier vase-and-ring turning style, plus the high H-stretcher arrangement, equals an excellent design. The seven finely shaped back spindles, turned in a simple bamboo pattern, swell slightly.

74

74.   Side chair. Probably New England; 1800–1820. Refinished; crest rail repaired. Crest rail and spindles, chestnut; back posts, legs, and stretchers, maple; seat, pine. SW 16½″, SD 14½″, SH 17½″, OH 36″. (Mr. and Mrs. R. W. P. Allen)

As much folk art as it is furniture, this is one of those fan-back Windsor chairs that defies identification. I admit that I have never seen anything like it. The back posts, turned and carved in a wonderfully imaginative way, have a shape that generally echoes that of the seat contour. And the seat, carved as it is, gives the impression of being made of some sort of pliable material. Strangely, the bracing spindles, shaped like the back posts, are socketed right into the back of the seat, which has no tailpiece. The comb-piece is beaded on the bottom edge and has two horns on top. The only ''normal'' features of this quirky chair are its legs, stretchers, and spindles.

SACK-BACK

~

CHAIRS

CHAPTER FOUR

Judging from the number of sack-back Windsors that have survived over the last two centuries, the form enjoyed great popularity. A closer look at the various types of sack-backs will shed some light on regional Windsor production in general.

Produced after 1760, the majority of sack-backs were made in Philadelphia and exported by the thousands to all the Colonies. Philadelphia sack-backs are so similar in design that it is difficult to attribute a chair to a maker unless the chair is branded. Many Philadelphia chairmakers worked for each other at one time or another, or worked in close proximity. From a purely business point of view, that was probably advantageous, since different shops could be called upon to fill a particularly large shipping order that one shop was unable to handle alone—without a noticeable difference among the products.

Philadelphia sack-backs influenced most Windsor-makers in other areas—primarily in one of three ways. First, in centers such as Boston and Wilmington, Delaware, many chairmakers made sack-back Windsors with turning patterns and bow shapes quite similar to those of the conservative Philadelphia Quaker sack-backs. Second, Windsor chairmakers in Connecticut embraced the sack-back design but made it their own, and in my experience the widest variety of sack-back patterns were produced in Connecticut. Finally, although New York did not produce nearly the quantity of sack-backs one might expect from such a large chairmaking center, the New York sack-backs, while similar to the Philadelphia model, almost always exhibit the wonderfully bulbous turning patterns also found on New York bow-backs and continuous-arm chairs. This seems to hold true for Rhode Island as well, although we do not have evidence of nearly as many Rhode Island sack-backs as bow-back armchairs. Like their Connecticut counterparts, Rhode Island chairmakers were servicing local needs, and their designs tended to take on characteristics that changed from county to county and even shop to shop within a small geographic region. For example, witness the wide-ranging influence of E. B. Tracy's designs on many Connecticut Windsor chairmakers.

As might be expected, as soon as a particular shop's designs caught on, other chairmakers would follow suit, producing what we would today call knock-offs of a similar design. Of course, the more successful a particular shop, the more apprentices it needs. Eventually, some of those apprentices go into business for themselves, taking with them the design and construction techniques they learned at the hand of the master craftsman.

75

75.   Armchair. Philadelphia, 1765–1780. Old shellac finish over traces of the original green paint. Crest rail and arms, oak; spindles, hickory; arm supports, legs, and stretchers, maple; seat, poplar. SW 21¼", SD 15¾", SH 17½", OH 38½". (James and Nancy Glazer)

We begin with this chair because it is the only sack-back Windsor I have ever seen with the cylinder-and-ball foot of the Philadelphia comb-back Windsor. That design fell out of favor when Windsors became a mass-market product, so we can speculate that this chair was a custom order. The piece shows all the characteristics of the designs of Joseph Henzey and was probably made by him (see figure 79).

76. Armchair, Philadelphia, 1765–1780. Nineteenth-century apple-green paint with red, blue, and gilt striping and decoration, over the original green. Crest rail and arms, oak; spindles, hickory; arm supports, legs, and stretchers, maple; seat, poplar. SW 21¾″. SD 16⁵⁄₁₆″, SH 17¾″, OH 38⅝″. (Also see color plate II.) (Privately owned)

This is a very fine, well-turned sack-back with a strong, heavy-gauge bow. The stocky leg turnings are like those found on Windsors branded by Francis Trumble. What makes the design work so well are the closely spaced spindles. The two short spindles behind the arm supports represent a feature almost always found on these nine-spindle chairs. Like most other Philadelphia chairs of the period, this one has two ring turnings on either side of the medial stretcher. The paint surface adds an extra dimension to the piece.

76

77

77. Armchair. Philadelphia, 1765–1780. Branded W[illiam] WID-DEFIELD. Original green paint. Crest rail and arms, oak; spindles and arm supports, hickory; seat, poplar; legs and stretchers, maple. SW 21⅝″, SD 16⅜″, SH 17½″, OH 37¾″. (Privately owned)

Here is a seven-spindle Philadelphia sack-back of the best quality. It has a scrolled, flat arm, as do most seven-spindle Philadelphia sack-backs, but it also has two short spindles behind the arm support, usually found only on nine-spindle chairs like figure 76. The teardrop-shaped turning at the base of the arm support is an attractive feature.

78. Armchair. Philadelphia, 1765–1780. Bow repaired. Nineteenth-century varnish over traces of the original green paint. Crest rail and arms, oak; spindles, hickory; arm supports, legs, and stretchers, maple; seat, poplar. SW 21¾″, SD 15¾″, SH 17″, OH 37″. (Anthony Leone)

   A well-proportioned chair, this is one of the type that was produced by the thousands in Philadelphia and exported. It is a good, solid, conservative Quaker product, not as bold as the preceding chairs and lacking the extra short spindle behind each arm support. The turning pattern of the arm supports is much more typical of the Philadelphia product.

79

78

79. Armchair. Philadelphia, 1765–1780. Bottoms of knuckles missing. Dark green paint over the original green. Crest rail and arms, oak; spindles, hickory; arm supports, legs, and stretchers, maple; seat, poplar. SW 20⅞″, SD 15½″, SH 17″, OH 38⅝″. (Privately owned)

   While this fine chair is not branded, it exhibits many details that mark it as a product of the shop of Joseph Henzey. Among these features: 1) there is a slight chamfer on either side of the bow about four to five inches before it enters the arm rail; 2) the bow enters the arm rail flush with the outside edges instead of in the center; 3) the outside scroll of the handholds is formed by the arm rail itself instead of being an applied addition; 4) double wedges instead of single are used in all wedge joints; 5) the second and third spindles from the left and right penetrate the bow; 6) the leg turnings have a long baluster and short taper; 7) the turnings are rather slender overall.

   Regrettably, the bottoms of the knuckles have fallen off, a problem I have seen on many Henzey chairs. The reason is that the bottoms of the knuckles on these chairs are held in place only with glue and a single nail through the center, an unfortunately weak construction method. One more nail would have prevented this problem.

81. Armchair. Lancaster County, Pennsylvania, 1780–1800. One of six. Traces of the original green paint. Crest rail, spindles, and arms, hickory; arm supports, legs, and stretchers, maple; seat, poplar. SW 20¼″, SD 15½″, SH 17½″, OH 37″. (John Bartram Association)

One of a set of six, this chair has the typical Lancaster County seat with a heavy chamfer on the sides and a generally elliptical shape that is flatter in the front and rounder in the back than the seats of similar Windsor chairs. The front of the seat has been carved into a very distinctive pommel. The spindles swell slightly, the arm rail is thick, and the bow is a bit crude. The leg splay is good. Note the absence of the usual collar on the turnings where the baluster enters the ring.

80. Armchair. Philadelphia, 1765–1780. Branded I. [John] B. ACKLEY. Late nineteenth-century dark red paint over the original green. Crest rail and arms, oak; spindles, hickory; arm supports, legs, and stretchers, maple; seat, poplar. SW 21¼″, SD 16″, SH 17¾″, OH 39″. (James and Nancy Glazer)

All the earmarks of the style of Joseph Henzey can be seen here, yet this typical Philadelphia sack-back is branded by another Philadelphian, John Ackley—proving, perhaps, that chairmakers who work in close proximity may adopt each other's styles. The chair is not typical of the Ackley shop, which seems to have produced far more bamboo-turned than vase-and-ring-turned sack-backs like this one.

82.   Armchair. Philadelphia, 1780–1800. Branded L[ewis] BENDER. Bottoms of knuckles missing. Two coats of original green paint. Crest rail and arms, oak; spindles, hickory; arm supports, legs, and stretchers, maple; seat, poplar. SW 20⅜″, SD 15″, SH 17″, OH 36½″. (Lawrence Teacher)

At first glance this chair might seem to fully exemplify the Philadelphia style—but its medial stretcher has arrows at either end, in the Lancaster County style.

82

83

83.   Armchair. Bucks County or Lancaster County, Pennsylvania, 1780–1800. Nineteenth-century brown varnish, over an ochre ground, over traces of the original black paint. Crest rail, arms, and spindles, hickory; handholds, oak; arm supports, legs, and stretchers, maple; seat, poplar. SW 20¼″, SD 15¾″, SH 16½″, OH 44½″. (Mr. and Mrs. R. W. P. Allen)

With the same type of medial stretcher as figure 82, this chair is overall further removed from the Philadelphia style. The tall bow has a squarish shape. The front leg turnings are similar to those of the rear legs, and the four legs are tapered, whereas most Lancaster County Windsors have front legs with blunt-arrow turnings and tapered rear legs (see figures 84 and 85).

84. Armchair. Lancaster County, Pennsylvania, 1765–1780. Refinished. Crest rail, spindles, and arms, hickory; handholds and seat, poplar; arm supports, legs, and stretchers, maple. SW 21¼″, SD 15⅞″, SH 15¾″, OH 42½″. (Privately owned)

This chair is much more typical of the Lancaster County product. However, sack-backs with such tall bows are a rare form. Many of them exhibit similarities, including the slightly pinched bow, which suggest that the chairs may all have been made in the same shop. The blunt-arrow foot, as opposed to a tapered foot, is a holdover from earlier Windsors. Lancaster County Windsors of this tall bow type usually have blunt-arrow front legs and tapered back legs; chairs with four blunt-arrow legs are more rare.

The Pennsylvania Germans were great cabinetmakers who loved to show, rather than hide, how their pieces were constructed. Thus, for example, the handholds are pinned in place with very large dowels. Note also the slightly swelling spindles.

84

85.   Armchair. Lancaster County, Pennsylvania. 1775–1790. Old refinishing with traces of the original green paint. Crest rail, oak; seat, poplar; spindles, hickory; arms, hickory or ash; handholds, arm supports, legs, and stretchers, maple. SW 21″, SD 15½″, SH 16½″, OH 35¼″. (Mr. and Mrs. Victor Johnson)

A well-proportioned Lancaster County Windsor, this armchair has exceptionally fine knuckles. The leg taper starts almost directly below the stretcher.

85

86

86.   Armchair. Lancaster County, Pennsylvania, 1760–1785. Old dark green paint over the original green. Top crest rail, hickory or oak; crest rail and handholds, oak; spindles and arms, hickory; arm supports, legs, and stretchers, maple; seat, poplar. SW 25½″, SD 23⅟₁₆″, OH 44⁹⁄₁₆″. (The Henry Francis du Pont Winterthur Museum)

This is a rare triple-back form of which I have seen only three Lancaster County examples. The top of the comb-piece echoes the wave beneath the comb. The leg and arm-support turnings are very crisply executed, and the turnings where the arm support enters the arm are narrow and delicate.

87.   Armchair. New York City, 1765–1780. Old black paint over traces of the original green. Crest rail and arms, oak; spindles, hickory; arm supports, legs, and stretchers, maple; seat, poplar. SW 20⅝″, SD 16⅛″, SH 16¾″, OH 36⅛″. (Janie and Dr. Peter Gross)

New York sack-backs are relatively rare—not nearly as numerous as sack-backs from Pennsylvania or Connecticut, for example. With its nine spindles, wonderfully bold turnings, and great presence, this is one of the best New York City sack-backs. Most of these chairs have flat arms, no knuckles and seats with no distinct pommel.

88.   Armchair. New York City or southern Connecticut, 1780–1800. Late-nineteenth-century green paint over the original salmon-color paint. Crest rail and arms, oak; spindles, hickory; arm supports, legs, and stretchers, maple; seat, pine. SW 21″, SD 15¼″, SH 18½″, OH 45½″. (Mr. and Mrs. R. W. P. Allen)

Highly stylized and unusual, this sack-back has typical New York City turnings on its legs, stretchers, and arm supports. The long back spindles are very delicate and flare out suddenly as they enter the seat, but the short spindles under the arms seem a bit heavy. The arm scroll is exaggerated, and the seat is imaginatively carved. Despite its New York turnings, the chair has an overall Connecticut look in its bow shape, arm rail, and the flat side of its seat.

87

88

89.   Armchair. New England, possibly Connecticut; 1790–1800. Branded O. NELSON. Varnish finish over green paint. Crest rail and spindles, hickory; arms, ash; arm supports, legs, and stretchers, maple; seat, pine. SW 20″, SD 13″, SH 17¼″, OH 38″. (Steven and Helen Kellogg)

The swell and sweep of this chair's bow can be found on other, similar Windsor chairs from Connecticut. This is an interesting, quirky piece with a very long reel on the leg turnings. Note how narrow the back spindles are at the seat and how they differ from the side spindles.

89

90

90.   Armchair. Connecticut, 1780–1800. Late nineteenth-century dark red paint over the original green paint, striped and decorated with gilt paint. Top crest rail and crest rail, oak; spindles and arms, ash; arm supports and stretchers, chestnut; seat, basswood; legs, maple. SW 20¼″, SD 16¼″, SH 17¼″, OH 44¼″. (Sam Bruccoleri)

Here is a great piece of Connecticut furniture and one very much like chairs that are known to come from the Westbrook area. Though the ears are typically Connecticut in design, all seven spindles penetrate the comb-piece, which is not typical. Another Connecticut feature is the fact that the medial stretcher has no double ring. The long taper of the arm supports is unusual. Although the legs have been notched out for rockers, this should not detract appreciably from the chair's value because the legs have not been cut down. The chair is decorated like mid-nineteenth-century "fancy" chairs.

91.   Armchair. New York, Albany area, 1780–1800. Branded S. N. HERRCK. (Sotheby's, Inc.)

New York chairs with idiosyncratic turnings often come from the Albany area. Signed by a Dutch maker, this piece shows a strong Dutch influence in its turning patterns. There is a nice swell in the leg turnings where the stretcher enters. All told, this is a well-proportioned, good variation on the conventional Windsor design.

92.   Armchair. Massachusetts, possibly Concord; 1790–1800. Early nineteenth-century green paint over the original salmon-color paint. Crest rail and arms, oak; handholds, cherry; spindles, hickory; arm supports, legs, and stretchers, maple; seat, chestnut. SW 21″, SD 16″, SH 18½″, OH 42″. (Nancy and Tom Tafuri)

In many ways, this chair is similar to figure 186. The seat is quite thick—3″—and well carved. The unusual leg turnings are also similar to those of figure 186. Oddly, the knuckle pieces are attached to the inside of the arms rather than the outside.

93

93.   Armchair. Connecticut, 1780–1800. Nineteenth-century red
paint over the original green. Crest rail and arms, oak; spindles, hickory; arm supports, legs, and medial stretcher, maple; seat and side
stretchers, chestnut. SW 21¼″, SD 15½″, SH 16¾″, OH 37″. (Nancy
and Tom Tafuri)

This is a beautifully proportioned chair with great splay and a
wonderful paint patina. The knuckles are very well carved and made
from a single piece of wood. All the long spindles penetrate the bow.
The legs do not penetrate the seat.

94. Armchair. Connecticut, 1790–1810. Early nineteenth-century black paint with gilt striping over blue paint, over the original green paint. Crest rail and arms, oak; spindles, hickory; arm supports, legs, and stretchers, maple; seat, pine. SW 20″, SD 15″, SH 17″, OH 37⅜″. (Nancy and Tom Tafuri)

Though simple in design, this chair has great provincial charm. The seat is very heavily chamfered, and the turnings are reminiscent of those found on certain tavern tables.

95

94

95. Armchair. Connecticut, 1790–1810. Very old dark brown paint over traces of the original gray-green. Top crest rail and stretchers, chestnut; crest rail and arms, oak; spindles and arm supports, hickory; seat, butternut; legs, chestnut (left side) and maple (right side). SW 21″, SD 14¾″, SH 16¼″, OH 51½″. (Kathleen Mulhern)

Both delicate and simple, this is an open, airy chair. The leg turnings—two balusters separated by a reel—are typical of Connecticut. The seat has been carved to almost a knife edge. Like that of figure 86, the bottom edge of the comb-piece conforms to the shape of the bow—a feature not always found on these chairs. (Compare the curve with that of figure 86.) The spindles penetrate the bottom of the seat. While the legs are turned from two different woods, they are original.

96

97

97.   Armchair. Lisbon, Connecticut, 1790–1803. Branded EB: TRACY. Refinished. Crest rail and arms, oak; spindles, hickory; arm supports and legs, maple; seat and stretchers, chestnut. SW 19¾", SD 15½", SH 16¾", OH 36½". (Joan and Don Mayoras)

With this chair begins what was to become a Connecticut chairmaking dynasty with far-reaching influence. This Ebenezer Tracy Windsor differs from other Connecticut Windsors in its abruptly swelling spindles; its distinctive seat shape and leg turnings; its thin medial stretcher with arrows; its arm supports, whose turning pattern differs from that of the legs; its chestnut seat; and its bow, which does not flatten out as it enters the arm rail but merely tapers. While this is not a knuckle armchair, Tracy produced them—and when he did, the side stretchers often have arrows like that of the medial stretcher in this example.

96.   Armchair. New England, possibly Connecticut; 1800–1810. Nineteenth-century salmon-color paint over the original green. Crest rail and arms, oak; spindles, hickory; arm supports, legs, and stretchers, maple; seat, pine. SW 21", SD 15⅞", SH 17¼", OH 36½". (Nancy and Tom Tafuri)

The leg turnings on this chair are quite simple, but that does not mean the chair is uninteresting. The chair has an unusually high stretcher arrangement that works quite well. The seat is not particularly well developed, with only a vague attempt at saddling. The legs do not penetrate the seat. The nineteenth-century salmon paint over the original green gives this piece a great deal of its charm.

98.   Armchair. Lisbon, Connecticut, 1795–1800. Branded E[lijah] TRACY. Refinished; traces of white, black, and the original green paint. Crest rail, oak; arms, ash; spindles, stretchers, and seat, chestnut; arm supports and legs, maple. SW 19½″, SD 15¼″, SH 16¾″, OH 35¾″. (Joan and Don Mayoras)

Out of the same shop as figure 97, this chair was possibly made by Ebenezer Tracy's son, Elijah. Overall, it is not quite as good as figure 97, especially in the arm supports.

99

98

99.   Armchair. Lisbon, Connecticut, 1790–1803. Original black paint with gilt striping. Crest rail, spindles, arm supports, and stretchers, hickory; arms, oak; seat, chestnut; legs, maple. SW 19½″, SD 15½″, SH 16″, OH 34¼″. (Steven and Helen Kellogg)

Though unbranded, this chair is so similar to the previous two examples that it almost certainly came from the Ebenezer Tracy shop. When Tracy used knuckles on his chairs, he also used side stretchers with arrow terminations, as in this chair; usually, when his chairs have flat scrolled arms, the side stretchers do not have arrows.

100

101

101. Armchair. Connecticut, 1796–1800. Early nineteenth-century mahoganizing over traces of the original black paint. Crest rail, spindles, and handholds, hickory; arms, oak; arm supports, legs, and side stretchers, maple; seat, chestnut; medial stretcher, birch. (Steven and Helen Kellogg)

This is a chair that may be attributable to A. D. Allen—but, I think, made after Allen left Ebenezer Tracy's shop to open his own. The chair retains the same basic design as figure 100, but the turning patterns have changed, the legs and stretchers no longer reflecting the Tracy design. For example, on each leg a rounded shoulder begins the taper below the ring. The turning pattern of the side stretchers flows more gradually, suggesting that Allen is now turning his own parts and not pulling them from the general Tracy stock. This chair also combines arrowed side stretchers with knuckle handholds, as does figure 99. While this is certainly a fine chair, the turnings are not the equal of Tracy's.

100. Armchair. Connecticut, 1796–1800. Branded A[mos] D[enison] ALLEN. Refinished. Crest rail, hickory; spindles, seat, and stretchers, chestnut; arms, oak; arm supports and legs, maple. SW 19½", SD 15", SH 16¼", OH 35¼". (Joan and Don Mayoras)

An apprentice to Ebenezer Tracy from 1790 to 1795, A. D. Allen eventually married Tracy's daughter Lydia and opened his own shop in 1796. In this chair we can see the influence of the Tracy style on Allen. There is a slight difference in the front of the seat: Allen carved his straight across, while Tracy undercut the seat from beneath. Like Tracy, Allen did not usually use arrows on the side stretchers of chairs with flat, scrolled arms.

102

103

102. Armchair. Connecticut, 1795–1800. Leather seat not original. Early nineteenth-century varnish with a salmon-color ground to simulate rosewood. Crest rail and arms, oak; spindles, ash; arm supports, chestnut; seat, pine; legs and stretchers, maple. SW 20½″, SD 16⅜″, SH 17″, OH 35⅝″. (Claude and Alvan Bisnoff)

Like the previous chair, this may also be an A. D. Allen product. On the other hand, it may only be a Tracy-influenced chair. The knuckles are very well executed. The seat shape is different from figure 101, and the stretchers have only rings, rather than the characteristic Tracy-Allen arrows at the ends. The leather cover of the seat is old, but not original. The knuckles on this chair are extremely bold.

103. Armchair. Massachusetts, 1780–1795. Original green paint over a gray ground. Crest rail and arms, oak; spindles, hickory; arm supports, chestnut; seat, legs, and stretchers, maple. SW 20¾″, SD 14⅝″, SH 17¾″, OH 38¾″. (Claude and Alvan Bisnoff)

The turnings on this chair are graceful, slender, and crisp. Note the tall back and how high the arm rail is from the seat.

104.

105. Armchair. Massachusetts, Boston area, 1780–1800. Branded [William] SEAVER. Original black paint over a gray ground. Crest rail and arms, oak; spindles and side stretchers, hickory; arm supports and medial stretcher, chestnut; seat, possibly maple; legs, maple. SW 19¾″, SD 14⅞″, SH 18¼″, OH 37″. (Claude and Alvan Bisnoff)

Some of the chairs made by William Seaver are wonderfully quirky. The abrupt bulbs in the spindles, the blocking in the legs before they enter the seat, and the medial stretcher with its ring-and-arrow design give this chair its stylistic personality.

104. Armchair. Massachusetts, 1780–1800. Red varnish over late nineteenth-century red paint, over the original green paint. Crest rail and arms, oak; spindles, hickory; arm supports, legs, and stretchers, maple; seat, pine. SW 20½″, SD 15⅜″, SH 17″, OH 36½″. (Nancy and Tom Tafuri)

This chair is similar to figure 103, but has somewhat more vigorous turnings. In fact, the turnings are like those found on the great tenon-arm fan-back Windsor chairs from eastern Massachusetts (see figures 63 and 64). The back has a nice little shoulder where the bow enters the armrail.

105

106A. Armchair. Detail of knuckles. The strange groove cut behind the knuckles must have had some use, but its purpose has been lost.

106A

106

106.   Armchair. Boston, 1780–1800. Refinished. Crest rail and arms, oak; spindles, ash; arm supports, legs, and stretchers, maple; seat, possibly butternut. SW 21¾″, SD 15¾″, SH 18″, OH 41″. (Joan and Don Mayoras)

Characteristic of a type of Boston product, this chair has a medial stretcher very similar to that of figure 105.

108. Armchair. Rhode Island, 1780–1800. Late nineteenth-century black paint with gilt striping. Crest rail and arms, oak; spindles, hickory; arm supports, legs, and stretchers, maple; seat, pine. SW 21¼″, SD 16″, SH 18½″, OH 38″. (Charles Sterling)

Here is a well-balanced sack-back with all the earmarks of the New York City influence on Rhode Island chairmakers. It does have a slightly softer turning pattern, and, of course, the typical Rhode Island leg taper.

107

107. Armchair. Rhode Island, 1780–1810. Green paint over nineteenth-century salmon-color paint, over the original green. Crest rail and arms, oak; spindles, hickory; arm supports, legs, and stretchers, maple; seat, pine. SW 20½″, SD 15½″, SH 18½″, OH 39½″. (James and Nancy Glazer)

This handsome chair has typically Rhode Island leg and medial stretcher turnings. Note how far back the arm support is positioned behind the front legs. It is unusual to find a sack-back in this form, which is much more common to bow-back armchairs or continuous-arm chairs from Rhode Island.

108

109. Armchair. Massachusetts or Rhode Island, 1780–1800. Old shellac refinish. Crest rail and arms, oak; spindles, ash; arm supports, legs, and stretchers, maple; seat, chestnut. SW 20″, SD 15⅛″, SH 18″, OH 38¼″. (Joan and Don Mayoras)

This chair seems to have a Connecticut influence, especially in its bow, seat carving, and arm supports. The finely executed legs are in the Rhode Island style, and the medial stretcher has a Massachusetts look. Perhaps the chair was made in Boston—influenced by Connecticut and Rhode Island.

110. Armchair. Massachusetts or Rhode Island, 1790–1810. Refinished; traces of old black paint. Crest rail, spindles, and arms, hickory; arm supports, legs, and stretchers, maple; seat, pine. SW 20″, SH 17″, OH 46″. (Privately owned)

The high, delicate bow and spindles of this chair make it a rare form.

109

110

111

112

112.   Armchair. New England, possibly Rhode Island; 1790–1820. Original dark blue paint. Crest rail, spindles, and arms, hickory; arm supports, legs, and stretchers, maple; seat, pine. SW 20″, SD 13″, SH 16″, OH 32″. (Marianne Clark)

Perhaps this chair was made by a country craftsman who did not specialize in Windsors. The leg turnings resemble those of many New England tavern tables with their ball feet. The arm supports are turned in a pattern like the arm supports and leg turnings found on Rhode Island low-back Windsors, which are in the English taste. The spindles start with a very low taper. This is a very animated country Windsor.

111.   Armchair. Rhode Island, possibly Newport; 1770–1800. Traces of red paint. Crest rail, oak; spindles, legs, and stretchers, chestnut; arm supports, maple and oak; seat, curly maple. SW 22″, SD 15″, SH 16½″, OH 36″. (David A. Schorsch, Inc.)

A strong English influence asserts itself in this chair, especially in the ram's-horn arm supports and Queen Anne medial stretcher. Such chairs are often mistaken for Pennsylvania products because of their D-shaped seats and blunt-arrow feet. This seat is made of curly maple. Newport chairs often are made entirely of one wood, and it is not unusual to find chairs in this style made completely from a single wood, often chestnut or maple. This is not so in Pennsylvania; the swelling in the spindles also is not found among Pennsylvania chairs.[4]

113. Armchair. Lancaster County, Pennsylvania, 1790–1810. Nineteenth-century black paint with gilt striping, over straw-color paint, over gray paint. Crest rail, hickory or oak; spindles and arms, hickory; handholds and seat, poplar; arm supports, legs, and stretchers, maple. SW 21½″, SD 16¼″, SH 18″, OH 41½″. (Wayne Pratt)

This is, in effect, a bamboo-turned version of many earlier Lancaster County sack-backs. Most interesting are the flared front feet, which follow the Lancaster County tradition of placing blunt-arrow feet in the front. In the typical late style, the knuckles are simplified and rolled over; they are made with three pieces added to the outside, inside, and underside. The second short spindle under each arm forms the same angle as the back spindles.

113

114

114. Armchair. Lancaster County, Pennsylvania, 1780–1800. Refinished; traces of the original green paint. Crest rail and arms, oak; spindles, hickory; handholds and seat, poplar; arm supports, legs, and stretchers, maple. SW 21⅜″, SD 16½″, SH 17¾″, OH 45¼″. (Mr. and Mrs. R. W. P. Allen)

Like figure 113, this is a bamboo-turned version of an earlier style. The chair has larger knuckles than those of figure 113. While the turning patterns of the legs and side stretchers can be found on many Philadelphia sack-backs—showing, perhaps, that the Lancaster chairmakers were paying attention to the Philadelphia products—the arm supports, high flat bow, slightly swelling spindles, and knuckle shape are pure Lancaster County.

BOW-BACK

~

CHAIRS

CHAPTER FIVE

In much the same way that the comb-back and low-back chairs became identified with Philadelphia in the 1750s, the bow-back also was a Philadelphia first. Based on an Oriental design that spread via England, the bow-back was introduced into Philadelphia in the 1780s when that city's chairmakers began producing bow-backs with bamboo turning patterns. This stylistic innovation was an immediate success and quickly became the Philadelphia chairmakers' most popular Windsor product, both locally and for export. From the mid-1780s through the 1790s, the New York makers, rather than imitate the Philadelphia product, created bow-backs with their own extraordinarily fine versions of the earlier vase-and-ring pattern.

Judging by the number of surviving New York bow-backs and the remarkable similarity in turning patterns and overall design among chairs by different makers—the crisp-edged, shield-shaped seat with sliding corners, the slightly swelling spindles, the relatively short back, and the like—the bow-back must have been immensely popular and a best-seller in New York, despite design changes in other Windsor production centers. Apart from its general excellence, another reason for its popularity may have been the fact that the bow-back made a perfect side chair for another Windsor form identified with New York—the continuous-arm chair. To be sure, New York bow-back armchairs exist, but they are very rare and have a curiously experimental look about them, with their stubby arms that seem almost out of place. To me that implies two things: the bow-back form as a whole probably preceded the continuous-arm chair, and the experiment of the bow-back armchair in New York City was quickly abandoned in favor of the far more elegant continuous-arm chair.

The New York influence spread to chairmaking shops primarily in Connecticut and Rhode Island. The Rhode Island makers, also influenced by Philadelphia, produced some of the best bow-back armchairs and side chairs, some of which have distinctively turned baluster spindles.

Most of the bow-backs produced in other areas—such as the rest of New England and the South—seem to have been mainly influenced by the Philadelphia model, the bamboo-turned bow-back side chair and armchair with arms attached by mortise-and-tenon joints. Indeed, it is quite likely that the New York continuous-arm chair was designed to compete with the Philadelphia tenon-arm bow-back. I base this on the fact that I have never seen a continuous-arm chair from Philadelphia, nor have I ever seen a bamboo-turned tenon-arm chair from New York.

Such steadfast adherence to certain regional designs may well have been a reflection of an unwritten rule or deliberate choice among Windsor makers to acknowledge their competition in other cities and demonstrate their pride in creating their own Windsor idioms.

115.   Armchair. Philadelphia, 1785–1800. Branded I. [John] B. ACKLEY. Traces of original mahoganizing. Crest rail, arms, and arm supports, oak; spindles, hickory or oak; seat, poplar; legs and stretchers, maple. SW 20¼″, SD 17¾″, SH 18″, OH 37¾″. (M. Finkel & Daughter)

If there were a typical Philadelphia bow-back armchair, this would be a good candidate to represent the many chairs of this style that were produced by most of the Windsor chairmakers of the period—including Henzey, Lambert, Trumbull, Pentland, Cox, and Allwine. This chair by J. B. Ackley is so similar to those produced by Henzey that it would be difficult to differentiate between them if the chair were not branded. The turning pattern of the side stretchers is especially typical of both Henzey and Ackley, although other makers used a similar pattern.

116

115

116.   Armchair. Philadelphia, 1780–1800. Punch marks of William Cox. Original mahoganizing over straw-color ground. Crest rail, spindles, arms, and arm supports, oak; seat, poplar; legs and stretchers, maple. SW 19¼″, SD 17½″, SH 17¼″, OH 37½″. (Michael McCue)

Somewhat more conservative than figure 115, this is another typical Philadelphia bow-back design that is even more commonly found.

117. Armchair. Philadelphia, 1785–1795. Punch marks of William Cox. One spindle missing. Nineteenth-century mahoganizing over original mahoganizing; original horsehair-stuffed muslin seat cushion; outer upholstery missing. Crest rail, oak; spindles, hickory; arms and arm supports, mahogany; seat, poplar; legs and stretchers, maple. SW 20″, SD 18″, SH 17″, OH 39″. (Privately owned)

Its upholstered seat makes this an interesting variation of the Philadelphia bow-back—and, indeed, simply an upholstered version of figure 116. The seat has been stripped of its original leather covering, which was wrapped around and tacked in place, and we can see the inner muslin cover stuffed with horsehair and nailed onto the thick, unsaddled plank seat. This chair has mahogany arms and arm supports—fine features—but the leg and stretcher turnings are rather bland when compared with the crisp, bulbous leg and stretcher turnings of figure 115.

118. Armchair. Philadelphia, probably 1792. One of 12. Original mahoganizing over buff-color ground. Crest rail, hickory; spindles, probably hickory; arms, mahogany; arm supports, oak; seat, poplar; legs and stretchers, maple. SW 21″, SD 16½″, SH 18½″, OH 38⅛″. (The Library Company of Philadelphia)

The minutes of the Library Company of Philadelphia for December 6, 1792, mention a dozen chairs that were purchased from Joseph Henzey. A set of 11 Windsors still remains in the Library Company—of which this is one—and these are believed to be the chairs mentioned in the minutes. Aesthetically, this chair ranks between figures 115 and 117 as an expression of the Philadelphia bow-back.

117

118

119

120

120.   Side chair. Philadelphia, 1785–1800. Branded LAMBERT. Old black paint over the original white; reupholstered. Crest rail, oak; spindles, hickory; legs and stretchers, maple. SW 18″, SD 16½″, SH 18″, OH 37″. (Also see color plates XI and XII.) (Privately owned)

Its upholstered seat makes this chair unusual, although it is similar to figure 115 in its legs and stretchers.

119.   Armchair. Philadelphia, 1780–1800. Refinished; traces of original yellow paint. Crest rail, center posts, splats, and arm supports, oak; spindles, legs, and stretchers, maple; arms, mahogany; seat, poplar. SW 20¾″, SD 16″, SH 17½″, OH 37⅜″. (Mr. and Mrs. R. W. P. Allen)

This is a ladder-back Windsor of the so-called Trotter type, a very rare form that was made in limited sets. It is practically identical to the three previous examples, with the exception of its ladder-back slats, which are no doubt derived from Philadelphia Chippendale formal chairs made by Daniel Trotter, Thomas Tufft, and others. Chairs with this kind of back arrangement and these curved arm supports are very English in character. A side chair version also exists.

121. Side chair. Philadelphia, 1780–1800. Branded W[illiam] BOWEN. Refinished; traces of red paint over the original green. Crest rail and spindles, oak; seat, poplar; legs and stretchers, maple. SW 17″, SD 16″, SH 18″, OH 37½″. (Mrs. Hazel Douglass)

Similar to figure 120 but with less pronounced turnings, this is a typical Philadelphia bow-back product with bamboo turnings, nine spindles, and pinched bow.

122

121

122. Side chair. Philadelphia, ca. 1791. Branded C[hristian] HEINY. Refinished; traces of black paint over the original green. Crest rail, oak; spindles, hickory; seat, poplar; legs and stretchers, maple. SW 17¼″, SD 16½″, SH 18″, OH 37″. (Mrs. Hazel Douglass)

Like figure 121, this chair is very similar to the typical Philadelphia product, but the proportions of its legs are more pleasing. Note the extra flare on the leg turning before it enters the seat and the fullness at the bottom of the leg where the side stretchers are socketed. The back is better as well because the spindles are thicker. Heiny is known to have worked in Philadelphia in 1791.

123. Pair of side chairs. Pittsburgh, 1780–1800. Branded T. RAMSEY/W. DAVIS/PITTSBURGH. Original black paint. Crest rails and spindles, hickory; seats, poplar; legs and stretchers, maple. SW 18″, SD 16″, SH 17″, OH 37″. (Tom Brown)

While Philadelphia chairmakers were producing bamboo turnings, Pittsburgh makers were still using vase-and-ring-turned legs and baluster side stretchers. However, the medial stretchers on these chairs are bamboo-turned. The backs, seats, and leg turnings are especially well executed. In fact, the chairs resemble those made by Henzey, but the balusters are shorter and the leg taper longer.

124

125

125. Side chair. Richmond, Virginia, 1790–1800. Label of Andrew and Robert McKim. Traces of black and yellow paint. Crest rail and spindles, hickory; seat, poplar; legs and stretchers, maple. SW 17″, SD 15¾″, SH 17¼″, OH 37½″. (Museum of Early Southern Decorative Arts, Winston-Salem, N.C.)

We know that many Windsors were shipped from Philadelphia to Richmond. Here is an example of a chair that was made in Richmond but which bears the unmistakable stamp of the Philadelphia stylistic influence in its seat shape, bamboo turnings, and the shaping of the bow. Compare this chair with figure 122, which has nine spindles, like most Philadelphia bow-backs.

124. Side chair. Philadelphia area, 1785–1800. Mid-nineteenth-century black paint with gilt striping, over earlier gray paint, over the original bronze-color paint. Crest rail, oak; spindles, hickory; seat, poplar; legs and stretchers, maple. SW 17¼″, SD 16½″, SH 16½″, OH 37⅜″. (Eugene Pettinelli)

Here is a provincial variant of chairs like figure 120. The chairmaker has attempted to turn the legs in proportion, but the result is somewhat clumsy. The tops of the legs are weak and club-shaped, and the seat saddling is vague. The back of the chair is more successful. Nonetheless, the chair is desirable because of its paint surface and its country charm.

126. Side chair. Berks County or Lancaster County, Pennsylvania, 1780–1800. Old red paint over the original green. Crest rail and spindles, hickory; seat, pine or poplar; legs and stretchers, maple. SW 17¼″, SD 16″, SH 19″, OH 39¼″. (Marianne Clark)

Chairs of such idiosyncratic stylishness often are provincial products. The finely saddled seat of this chair has an almost sculptural quality, and the leg turnings are very beautiful. The stretchers are turned in a pattern typical of the area. The pinched waist of the bow is a nice touch.

127. Armchair. Frederick-Hagerstown (Piedmont) area of Maryland, 1790–1810. Very old brown paint over the original red. Crest rail, oak or hickory; spindles and arm supports, hickory; arms, legs, and stretchers, maple; seat, poplar. SW 19⁵⁄₁₆″, SD 16¹¹⁄₁₆″, SH 15¾″, OH 35¼″. (Museum of Early Southern Decorative Arts, Winston-Salem, N.C.)

This chair descended in the Taney family of the Frederick-Hagerstown area of Maryland. The shaping of the arms and the carving of the knuckles is an exaggeration of the Chippendale style and a very lively conceit. Note the especially low seat (less than 16″), the severe bend in the "wrist" of the arm, and the pinched bow—the latter a motif seen much more often in side chairs than in armchairs. All these features appear on other Windsors found in the same area.

127A. Armchair. Detail of arm.

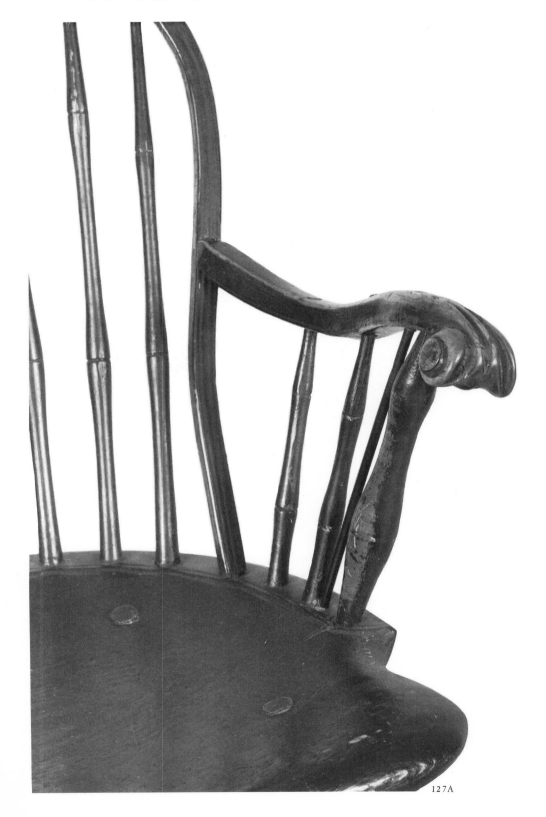

127A

128.   Side chair. Frederick-Hagerstown (Piedmont) area of Maryland, 1790–1810. Late nineteenth-century varnish over traces of the
original white paint. Crest rail, probably oak; spindles, hickory; seat,
pine; legs and stretchers, maple. SW 17¼″, SD 16⅞″, SH 16¼″, OH
36¼″. (Privately owned)

Overall, this chair is a marvelous regional variant of the
bamboo-turned Windsors produced in Philadelphia. The turner
incorporated the new bamboo motif into his turning patterns without completely dismissing the earlier baluster turnings. The seat is
beautifully saddled, and the lower spindle turnings are echoed in the
tops of the legs. I have seen several side chairs like this one, and all are
relatively low to the ground—that is, not cut down.[5]

129. Armchair. New York City, 1780–1795. Nineteenth-century varnish over the original red paint. Crest rail and arms, oak; spindles, hickory; arm supports, legs, and stretchers, maple; seat, pine or poplar. SW 18¼", SD 17½", tailpiece 3¾", SH 17", OH 36". (Privately owned)

In New York, and north into New England, bow-backs were still being made with vase-and-ring turnings rather than bamboo turnings at a rather late date. These New York and New England chairs often have braced backs, whereas Philadelphia bamboo-turned chairs almost never do. This is a very fine chair of a rare type with short, mortised arms. Indeed, the arms are like those one would expect to find on a sack-back Windsor, but cut off abruptly. Occasionally chairs like this one have flaring arms with well-carved knuckles, but they are an even rarer form. The vase-and-ring turnings shown here are very bold, and so typical of the New York City style.

129A. Armchair. Detail of seat. Also typical of the New York City style is the very pronounced shield-shaped seat, bolder in its contours than its Philadelphia counterparts.

130

130.   Side chair. New York City, 1780–1800. Label of Thomas and William Ash. One of a pair. Two coats of original green paint. Crest rail, ash; spindles, probably hickory; seat, pine; legs and stretchers, maple. SW 16½″, SD 17½″, tailpiece 3¾″, SH 18″, OH 38½″. (Privately owned)

The best turning pattern of New York City bow-back Windsors is beautifully exemplified in this chair. Most New York City bowbacks are braced and do not have pinched waists.

131.   Side chair. New York City, 1780–1800. Nineteenth-century dark red paint over a salmon ground, over the original green paint. Crest rail, oak; spindles, hickory; seat, pine; legs and stretchers, maple. SW 16¾″, SD 17¾″, SH 18″, OH 38″. (Sam Bruccoleri)

Similar in expression to figure 130, this design features slightly bolder turnings.

132.   Side chair. New York City, 1790–1800. Branded I. [John] SPROSON. Painted black. Crest rail and spindles, hickory; seat, pine; legs and stretchers, maple. SW 16¼″, SD 17¼″, tailpiece 2½″, SH 18″, OH 35½″. (Mr. and Mrs. R. W. P. Allen)

This is an excellent braced bow-back from New York City with the best turnings and a finely saddled seat. Although practically identical to figures 130 and 131, this chair has legs with a slightly longer taper (however, this is not because the legs of the others have been cut down, since all three chairs have a seat height of 18″). The back of this chair is shorter than those of figures 130 and 131, and the spindles fan out more. Since the bow of figure 130 is higher, its back has a more vertical feeling.

Unfortunately, this chair has been repainted. Figure 131 has a nineteenth-century dark red paint over a salmon ground over the original green, which is a more desirable surface because it is closer to the original. But figure 130 is in even more pristine condition, with two coats of original green paint in virtually untouched condition; thus in my opinion it is the most desirable of the three chairs because of its surface condition, its Ash label, its taller back, and the fact that it is one of a pair.

133

134.   Side chair. New York City, 1780–1800. Nineteenth-century dark red paint with gilt striping over the original moss-green paint. Crest rail, oak; spindles, hickory; seat, pine; legs and stretchers, maple. SW 17½″, SD 17½″, tailpiece 2⅝″, SH 15½″, OH 34¾″. (Janie and Dr. Peter Gross)

Although not quite as well proportioned as figure 133, this chair is a good example of the New York City Windsor style. The leg turnings are somewhat overpowered by the deeply carved saddle seat. Furthermore, its more interesting paint surface makes this chair desirable from a collector's point of view.

133.   Side chair. New York City, 1790–1800. Branded W[illiam] MacBRIDE/N-YORK. Refinished; traces of the original green paint. Crest rail and spindles, hickory; seat, pine; legs and stretchers, maple. SW 14¾″, SD 17¼″, tailpiece 3″, SH 17¼″, OH 36⅝″. (Bernard & S. Dean Levy, Inc.)

Here is another well-turned, rather typical New York City braced bow-back side chair. The turnings are bold and well defined, but unfortunately, the chair has been skinned and refinished.

134

135

136. Side chair. Connecticut, 1790–1800. Label of William Harris, New London. Refinished. Crest rail, oak; spindles, ash; seat, pine; legs and stretchers, maple. SW 15¾″, SD 16½″, tailpiece 2¾″, SH 18″, OH 36″. (Dietrich American Foundation)

This is a good example of the Connecticut version of the New York City bow-back chair. The seat is narrower than those of New York examples, and the top is a little light in relation to the undercarriage; this might be the result of its having seven spindles instead of the more usual nine. It's a nice chair, however, and a type that was more popular in New York City than in Connecticut, judging from the number of surviving examples with New York brands or labels.

136

135. Side chair. New York or Connecticut, 1780–1800. One of a pair. Two coats of green paint over nineteenth-century salmon paint, over the original green. Crest rail, oak; spindles, oak or ash; seat, pine or poplar; legs and stretchers, maple. SW 16⅛″, SD 17″, tailpiece 3⅜″, SH 17″, OH 36″. (Sam Bruccoleri)

The slight swelling of the spindles of this chair, which occurs gradually from bottom to top, seems to be a New York feature—differing from the abrupt, bulbous swelling of Connecticut Windsors (see figures 98, 99, and 100). The swelling spindles, strong turnings, heavy bow, and broad, fully sculpted shield-shaped seat could be viewed as an attempt by a Connecticut maker to create a New York-style bow-back Windsor. While this is a fine chair, it does lack the sophistication of figures 130, 131, and 132.

137.   Armchair. Rhode Island, 1790–1800. One of a pair. Late nineteenth-century black paint over the original green, over a gray ground. Crest rail and spindles, hickory; arms, mahogany; arm supports, chestnut; seat, pine; legs and stretchers, maple. SW 18½″, SD 17¾″, tailpiece 2¾″, SH 17¾″, OH 39⅛″. (Claude and Alvan Bisnoff)

    A beautiful example of Rhode Island chairmaking, this chair has typical Rhode Island turnings, pipestem spindles, a high back, and wonderfully curved mahogany arms. Its paint sequence is very common to Rhode Island Windsors.

137

138. Armchair. Rhode Island, 1800–1810. Refinished. Crest rail and spindles, ash; arms, mahogany; arm supports, legs, and stretchers, maple; seat, pine. SW 16½″, SD 16⅜″, SH 17¾″, OH 38½″. (Joan and Don Mayoras)

The most obvious evidence for this chair's late date is the bamboo-turned medial stretcher. It's not a replacement, since it has the identical heavy decorative scoring that appears on the legs and side stretchers. The side stretchers have a late baluster shape, and the seat is shaped like those found on rod-back Windsors—i.e., a simplified shield. The spindles are no longer of the pipestem variety. This is a nice chair, but not as well realized as figure 137, to which it is somewhat similar.

139. Side chair. Rhode Island, 1790–1800. Refinished. Crest rail and spindles, hickory; seat, pine; legs and stretchers, maple. SW 16½″, SD 16¼″, tailpiece 2″, SH 17¾″, OH 37½″. (Dietrich American Foundation)

This is a side chair version of figure 137. The undercarriage is quite beautiful, but without the pipestem spindles in the back, the top of the chair doesn't live up to the undercarriage.

140

140.   Side chairs. Newport, Rhode Island, 1790–1800. Three of a set
of six. Nineteenth-century black paint with yellow, white, green, and
gilt decoration over the original blue-green paint. Crest rails and
spindles, ash; seats, pine; legs and stretchers, maple. SW 15¾″, SD
19¼″, SH 18½″, OH 39¼″. (David A. Schorsch, Inc.)
      More than any other bow-back Windsors, these chairs have
backs that could be called balloon-shaped. Note how the spindles
look like a unit in the center of the bow and how the pipestem turnings of the spindles are set high. The seats are thick but crisply carved
and saddled. The legs and stretchers are turned in the best Rhode
Island pattern. The medial stretchers are unusual.

141. Side chair. Massachusetts, probably Boston area; 1790–1810. One of six. Nineteenth-century varnish over traces of the original black paint. Crest rail and spindles, hickory; seat, pine; legs and side stretchers, maple; medial stretcher, chestnut. SW 16″, SD 16″, SH 18½″, OH 38½″. (Claude and Alvan Bisnoff)

The undulating spindles of this chair are a very interesting accomplishment, unifying the design of the undercarriage with the back of the chair. The leg turnings represent a variation of the Rhode Island style, and their vase-and-ring pattern blends nicely with the later style of the bamboo-turned spindles and medial stretcher because of the additional swelling in the center of each bamboo spindle.

141

142. Side chair. Boston, 1790–1810. Original yellow paint with black decoration. Crest rail, oak; spindles and bowed stretcher, hickory; seat, pine; legs and rear stretchers, maple. SW 17¼″, SD 16½″, SH 17½″, OH 37½″. (Mr. and Mrs. R. W. P. Allen)

The yoke stretcher arrangement of this chair, common on English Windsors, is a rarity among American Windsors and does not seem to have been popular in this country. It is most often seen among chairs from the Boston area, especially those made by Seaver and Frost, and seems always to appear on bow-backs, almost always side chairs. This chair is a graceful example of the type. Note how similar the spindles are to those of figure 141—bamboo turnings with an extra swelling between the two score marks. This is typical of many of these chairs from the Boston area.

143. Side chair. Massachusetts, probably Boston area; 1790–1810. Old black paint over nineteenth-century red paint. Crest rail and spindles, hickory; seat, pine; legs and stretchers, maple. SW 18″, SD 15¾″, SH 21¼″, OH 40″. (Mr. and Mrs. R. W. P. Allen)

Exceptionally tall for a bow-back side chair, this chair may have been used for a particular purpose, perhaps as a musician's seat. Note the similarity in the leg turnings to those of figure 142—the blocking and the concavity below it—and the slight flaring of the spindles just before they enter the seat. The chair also has a pinched waist and the same form of shield-shaped seat.

144. Side chair. Boston, 1790–1810. Branded S[amuel] J. TUCKE. Very old light blue paint, over beige paint, over the original green. Crest rail, oak; spindles, hickory or ash; seat, pine; legs and stretchers, maple. SW 15⅛″, SD 16″, SH 17¼″, OH 30″. (Privately owned)

The unfinished pine seat of this chair has the mellow color of wood that has never been painted, and it is peppered with tack holes—evidence that the seat originally was upholstered. The spindles flare slightly before they enter the seat, as in figures 142 and 143, and there also is a similarity in the block stretcher and leg turnings of figure 143.

The very short back and upholstered seat indicate, I think, that the chair originally was designed for the workplace, perhaps as a loom or spinning-wheel chair. In any case, the form is rare: I have seen only a handful of Windsors with such short backs.

143

144

145

145.   Armchair. Connecticut, 1790–1800. Late nineteenth-century dark red paint over the original green. Crest rails, spindles, and arm supports, hickory; arms, legs, and stretchers, maple; seat, poplar. SW 18″, SD 17″, SH 17¼″, OH 45″. (Privately owned; courtesy of Federation Antiques, Inc.)

Bow-backs with comb-pieces are rare. Sometimes the comb-piece, though always a welcome addition, seems to be merely a tacked-on afterthought; not so here. This bow-back has actually been designed to have a comb-piece. We can say that with some authority because, without the comb-piece, the back of this chair would appear too short; with the comb-piece, the proportions seem just right. In addition, the turnings are very well balanced. Unfortunately, the seat shows virtually no saddling.

146.   Side chair. New England, possibly Rhode Island; 1790–1800. Original black paint with gilt decoration over a white ground. Comb-piece, chestnut; crest rail, probably oak; spindles, hickory; seat, pine; legs and stretchers, maple. SW 16½″, SD 16½″, SH 17½″, OH 46¾″. (Privately owned)

The added comb-piece raises what might have been an ordinary chair to a high level of visual excitement. Note also that the maker chose to support the comb with six spindles instead of the usual three or five; thus the comb could be made wider and more imposing. This chair may be from Rhode Island because the ears of Rhode Island chairs usually have longer necks than those of chairs from other regions, as do these.

146

147

147.   Armchair. Philadelphia, 1785–1800. Refinished; traces of white paint. Crest rail and spindles, hickory; arms, mahogany; arm supports, legs, and stretchers, maple; seat, poplar. SW 19½″, SD 17¾″, SH 18″, OH 37¾″. (Privately owned)

Here we see a rare form—no doubt an attempt to emulate the shield-back formal chairs of the Hepplewhite style. This design would have been very successful had the back been made taller. As it is, we are left with the impression that the arms are set too high. Also, the legs and stretchers are a bit plain. Still, the rarity of the piece makes it desirable.

CONTINUOUS-ARM

~

CHAIRS

CHAPTER SIX

The continuous-arm Windsor chair has been something of a mystery in the world of early American furniture. While other Windsor forms—the comb-back, low-back, fan-back, sack-back, and bow-back—can be traced to English models from paintings, advertisements, inventories, wills, and surviving examples, the continuous-arm chair appears to have no English Windsor prototype in the eighteenth century, and has been called a true American invention.

Having thought about the matter for many years—and having done a little digging—I have now developed a theory of the origin of the form which identifies its prototype and its approximate time of development, and confirms that the form is, if not a totally American invention, at least an American innovation.

It was in the mid-1780s in New York City that several developments in furniture fashion probably inspired Windsor-makers there to create the continuous-bow armchair. First, although the Hepplewhite and Sheraton styles were the dominant forces in American furniture design from 1785 to 1800, the French taste was becoming popular in urban furniture-making centers. Boston, Philadelphia, and New York chairmakers were producing furniture in styles from Louis XVI designs to neoclassic designs inspired by French archaeological discoveries at the close of the eighteenth century. The fact that elliptical and circular shapes were mainstays in the vocabulary of these new French designs suggested new problems of construction for translating these flowing neoclassic styles into a back-and-arm construction for Windsor chairs.

The techniques of bending wood were not new to Windsor craftsmen, whose bow-back chairs were the height of fashion after 1780, particularly those chairs produced in Philadelphia with the newest simulated bamboo-style turnings. There had been a marked increase during the second half of the eighteenth century in patents for applying bent wood to manufactures, and Windsor craftsmen would naturally have been taking notice. In 1769 Joseph Jacob received an English patent for constructing wheel carriages "with hoop wheels."[6] One of the first recorded experiments in bending wood took place in Paris in 1778 at the shop of M. Migneron: observers saw "with astonishment" wood treated in some manner whereby it could be bent into different shapes and strengthened at the same time. M. Migneron's discovery was submitted to the Academies of Science and Architecture at Paris, Bordeaux, and Toulouse, and Benjamin Franklin was among the many distinguished inventors and artists to view this discovery.[7]

Similar ideas for the bending of wood soon appeared elsewhere. In 1791 a John Bevans took out a patent for "circular wooden sash frames, sashes and soffits; fanlight door mouldings and handrails for stairs" made from bent wood.[8] Samuel Bentham obtained an English patent dated April 23, 1793, for "giving curvature to wood by bending."[9]

Interest in these new wood-bending techniques was running high among the furniture craftsmen of New York, and among Windsor-chairmakers in particular, since they were then producing bow-backs and the earlier sack-back style, as were their Philadelphia counterparts. Competition between Windsor-chairmakers in New York and Philadelphia must have been keen, and I believe not without elements of regional pride. Whereas the simulated bamboo-turned bow-back accounted for at least ninety percent of the bow-back styles produced in Philadelphia, New York chairmakers seem to have ignored the style altogether; they seem to have preferred the turning patterns already in use on their earlier Windsor products. Nevertheless, the bow-backs of both New York and Philadelphia were basically the same: a steam-bent bow, socketed into the seat with seven or nine spindles.

It is when we look closely at the armchair versions of these New York and Philadelphia bow-backs that we see the greatest similarity and the greatest differences: similarity of purpose in the creation of an arm-and-back construction that achieves through design a continuity of line in keeping with the new classical influences; and differences in the way this design concept is achieved.

Philadelphia chairmakers were content to use a mortise-and-tenon joint to attach the arms to the bow. This form of arm-and-back construction, a traditional method, had been in use for formal Philadelphia chairs for some time. The illusion of the bow and arms of a bow-back Windsor being formed from a single piece of wood is created by using arms cut in the same thickness as the bow; by adding to the top surface of the arms a decorative beading that runs in a continuous line up onto the front facing of the bow; and by rounding the bow below the tenon of the arm and scoring it to resemble scored, bamboo-turned spindles.

There was a short-lived attempt among some New York City Windsor chairmakers to make a tenon-arm bow-back version of their own (see figure 129).[10] The design of these chairs was not very successful; there is no attempt to create the illusion of continuity between the bow and the arms, and the arms have a "stuck-on" look. Chairs of this type are quite rare. It does not appear that many of these tenon-arm chairs were produced; the design probably was quickly discarded in favor of a more successful and ultimately more popular design: the continuous-bow armchair.

New York City Windsor chairmakers succeeded in their attempt to bend the bow and arms from a single strip of wood, and for the first time outdid their Philadelphia competitors. Until the creation of the continuous-bow armchair, the New York City chairmakers were followers, producing sack-backs and other Windsor forms that already had been defined by the Philadelphia Windsor makers. Now, at last, a truly New York Windsor!

I think it is interesting to note that Philadelphia chairmakers did not produce continuous-arm Windsors, and New York City chairmakers as a rule did not produce the bow-back, bamboo-turned, tenon-arm counterparts. New York City Windsor-maker John Sproson, who made some of the finest continuous-arm chairs, did work in Philadelphia from 1783 to 1788, but he did not brand his chairs while working in that city. His branded continuous-arm chairs are New York in style and no doubt date from 1789 to 1798, when he had moved from Philadelphia and was living and working in New York City.

The identity of the first New York City Windsor chairmakers to produce a continuous-arm Windsor probably will never be determined with any certainty, but the brothers Thomas and William Ash probably are strong contenders for that honor. Born into a tradition of formal furniture-making, they were sons of Gilbert Ash (1717–1785), one of

New York City's most outstanding makers of Chippendale-style furniture, particularly chairs. Thomas and William Ash were both actively producing Windsors between 1785 and 1794. The following advertisement appeared in the *New York Packet* March 3, 1785:

> Thomas and William Ash, Windsor-chairmakers, No. 17 John Street . . . Now ready at the Ware-house, a great number of very neat chairs and settees, some of which is [*sic*] very elegant, being stuffed in the seat and brass nailed, a mode peculiar to themselves and never before executed in America.[11]

I have seen an example of an upholstered Ash continuous-bow armchair which, with the addition of brass nails, would indeed be very elegant and would bear a remarkable resemblance to a type of formal Federal upholstered armchair popular at that time known as a bergère-type chair. The similarities to a continuous-arm chair are especially noticeable in the flowing curve of the back into the arms. A labeled example of this type was produced in New York City in 1797 by John DeWitt and upholstered by William Gallatian.[12] Seven years earlier, in 1790, Thomas Burling, a New York City maker of formal furniture, produced a unique, swivel version of the bergère form for George Washington (figure 148). Thomas Jefferson, who had returned from his five-year mission to France the previous year, purchased a similar chair from Burling in 1790. America was closely affiliated with France at the close of the eighteenth century, and French-style furniture was popular with American political leaders. The fact that both Washington and Jefferson previously made other furniture purchases from Burling suggests Burling's prominence as a furniture maker.

The bergère form was very popular in formal furniture centers in Federal America. In 1797, George Bright of Boston produced thirty of these chairs, upholstered and brass-nailed, for the Boston State House.[13]

Could the Ash brothers, coming from a formal furniture background and armed with the most sophisticated recent information from abroad on wood-bending techniques, have seen the elegant bergère design as the best solution for putting arms on a bow-back Windsor chair? Mention has been made in the past of the stylistic similarities between one of the labels used by Thomas and William Ash and the label engraved for cabinetmaker Thomas Burling by Abraham Godwin of Paterson, New Jersey, who was trained in New York.[14] It is interesting to note that in accordance with their formal furniture background, Thomas and William Ash used labels rather than brands to identify their products, a practice not common among Windsor chairmakers in New York or Philadelphia.

The continuous-arm chair seems to have been an immediate success, and New England chairmakers soon were producing their own versions, but the New York influence is always evident in the turning patterns, the seat shape, and the overall rakish elegance of these chairs. With the development of this new Windsor form, New York City became as great an influence on the American Windsor market in the 1790s as Philadelphia had been in the previous decades.

148. Swivel armchair of the bergère type. New York, New York, 1790. Made by Thomas Burling for George Washington. Original upholstery. (Mount Vernon Ladies' Association)

148

149. Armchair. New York City, 1792. Branded [Abraham] HAMTON & [James] ALWAYS. Nineteenth-century dark green paint over the original green. Crest rail, oak; spindles, hickory; arm supports, legs, and stretchers, maple; seat, pine. SW 18″, SD 17½″, SH 18″, OH 36¼″. (Rosemary Beck and Ed Rogers)

A classic example of the highly sophisticated and ingenious continuous-arm chair first introduced by New York City chairmakers, this chair displays all the characteristic features, including bulbous, almost explosive turnings; a sharply chamfered, shield-shaped seat; a long leg taper; and nine nearly vertical spindles flanked by two short spindles.

149

150.

151. Armchair. New York City, 1785–1800. Branded W. Mac-BRIDE/N-YORK. Refinished; traces of the original blackish-green paint. Crest rail, oak; spindles, hickory; arm supports, legs, and stretchers, maple; seat, pine. SW 17″, SD 17½″, SH 17¾″, OH 38⅞″. (Bernard & S. Dean Levy, Inc.)

This handsome chair has more successfully turned arm supports than those of figure 150. The seat, while nearly identical, has a slight depression behind the pommel—a nice touch. The leg turnings are very well balanced and dynamic, and are matched by equally dynamic side and medial stretchers, which in figure 150 are something of a letdown. The greatest flaw in this chair is its highly refinished surface.

151.

150. Armchair. New York City, 1785–1800. Crest rail and spindles, oak; arm supports, legs, and stretchers, maple; seat, pine. SW 17¾″, SD 18″, SH 18¼″, OH 36¾″. (Joan and Don Mayoras)

Similar to figure 149, this New York armchair exhibits minor differences: the leg taper is not as long, so the chair is slightly less dramatic, and the top turning on the leg under the seat is a bit more bulbous—perhaps too bulbous.

152. Armchair. New York, possibly Albany area; 1790–1810. Painted black. Crest rail, oak; spindles, hickory; arm supports, legs, and stretchers, maple; seat, pine. SW 17½", SD 18", tailpiece 3¼", SH 18", OH 37½". (Mr. and Mrs. R. W. P. Allen)

At first glance, this braceback chair may seem to be a typical New York City product, but I think the slight rigidity of the leg turning pattern—without the thicks and thins of the previous examples—as well as a certain thickness in the front edge of the seat, and the heavy top baluster of the arm support, give the chair an air of provincialism. Nonetheless, it is a handsome piece. J. M. Hasbrouck produced similar chairs in the Albany area.

152

153

153. Armchair. New York, 1785–1810. Nineteenth-century black varnish over the original green paint with gilt striping. Crest rail, oak; spindles, hickory; arm supports, legs, and stretchers, maple; seat, pine. SW 17¾", SD 17⅛", SH 18¾", OH 37½". (Rosemary Beck and Ed Rogers)

Like figure 152, this chair lacks the sophistication of New York City continuous-arm Windsors. There is a slight thickness to the front chamfer of the seat, and the top balusters of the arm supports seem too small (just the opposite of figure 152). Also, the side stretchers are too bulbous for the thickness of the legs. This is a good attempt at a New York City chair, but it doesn't quite hit the mark. However, it does have a wonderful paint surface.

154. Armchair. New York, 1785–1800. Late nineteenth-century black paint with gilt striping over the original green paint. Crest rail, oak; spindles, hickory; arm supports, legs, and stretchers, maple; seat, poplar or pine. SW 17¾″, SD 17″, tailpiece 3″, SH 16⅛″, OH 34¼″. (Philip Bradley Antiques)

The turnings of this chair are beautifully executed, but the chair as a whole has a quiet, almost passive quality. The seat carving is a bit clumsy; the legs and arm supports do not splay very much; the bow does not have much bend; and the handholds are not scrolled. The chair does have a very pleasing paint surface.

155

154

155. Armchair. Probably Connecticut; 1790–1810. Early nineteenth-century white paint with gilt striping over the original green paint. Crest rail and spindles, ash; arm supports, legs, and stretchers, maple; seat, poplar. SW 16½″, SD 17″, SH 17″, OH 35½″. (David A. Schorsch, Inc.)

This is probably a Connecticut version of a New York City chair. The turnings do not have the thicks and thins typical of New York chairs, especially evident in the arm supports. The medial stretcher has no double rings. The handholds are quite thick and do not have chamfer on their underside, as New York chairs usually do. The seat is well saddled but not as heavily chamfered or refined as those of the New York City product. The bow is slightly more peaked than those of New York chairs. Overall, the chair has a wonderful stance, and its surface is enhanced by early nineteenth-century white paint with gilt striping over the original green.

156. Armchair. Connecticut, 1790–1800. Nineteenth-century dark brown paint over the original green. Crest rail and arm supports, oak; spindles, hickory; seat, pine; legs and stretchers, maple. SW 17¼″, SD 18″, tailpiece 3″, SH 18″, OH 40″. (Lori and Craig Mayor)

A far more typical Connecticut product than figure 155, this is similar to chairs made by Ebenezer Tracy[15] and clearly reveals the difference between the Connecticut and New York styles.

The general stance and splay are comparable, but the backs of Connecticut chairs are usually higher—in this case 40″, compared with New York chairs whose backs are usually 37″ or less in height. The Connecticut bow is narrower, and there is a more abrupt lift from the bend of the arm to the handhold. Connecticut chairs have spindles that distinctly swell about one-third their height from the seat. The Connecticut seat is different, as well: the legs do not penetrate the seat; the seat is usually made of a hardwood such as chestnut (although in this case the seat is pine); there is no scoring or "rain gutter" on the top back of the seat in front of the spindles, and the chamfering on the sides and front of the seat is usually very sharp and flat. The arm support and leg turning patterns tend to be slimmer but with a much wider reel than that of New York chairs. The medial stretcher has no ring on either side of its bulbous turning.

156

157

157.   Armchair. Massachusetts, 1790–1810. Old varnish or shellac over traces of dark green paint. Crest rail, oak; spindles, hickory; arm supports, legs, and stretchers, maple; seat, pine. SW 17½", SD 17½", SH 17⅛", OH 35⅞". (Mr. and Mrs. R. W. P. Allen)

This is a highly idiosyncratic chair. It has blocked bamboo turnings like those found on certain other Massachusetts Windsors (see, e.g., figures 142 and 143). The bow has an interesting squareness. Knuckle handholds are very rare on continuous-arm chairs, and these are cut from a single piece of wood.

158.   Armchair. Connecticut, 1790–1810. Feet repaired. Refinished. Top crest rail, arm supports, legs, and stretchers, maple; crest rail, oak; spindles, hickory; seat, pine. SW 17¾", SD 18", SH 16¾", OH 44¼". (Privately owned)

The bow of this chair is rather square, like that of figure 157; however, here the squareness seems appropriate because of the added and very appealing comb-piece, which is supported by the five longest spindles penetrating the bow. As is true of most Connecticut chairs, there is no double ringing on the medial stretcher. Overall, the chair has a pleasingly rustic quality.

158

159. Armchair. Probably Massachusetts; 1790–1800. Late nineteenth-century black paint over the original green. Crest rail, ash; spindles, hickory; arm supports, legs, and stretchers, maple; seat, chestnut. SW 16½″, SD 17½″, SH 18″, OH 35½″. (Mr. and Mrs. R. W. P. Allen)

Both the New York and Connecticut styles seem to have influenced this interesting Windsor. The turnings resemble those of New York Windsors, except for the blocking of the stretchers. While the spindles do not swell like those of Connecticut chairs, the back does have eight spindles—a hallmark of many chairs produced by Connecticut maker Ebenezer Tracy. Like the seats of many Connecticut Windsors, this one is made of chestnut and has a Connecticut shape, but it retains the rain gutter, and the legs penetrate the seat.

160

159

160. Armchair. Rhode Island, 1785–1800. Late nineteenth-century black paint over blue paint, over the original green. Crest rail, hickory; spindles, probably hickory; arm supports, legs, and stretchers, maple; seat, pine. SW 17⅜″, SD 18″, SH 18″, OH 37½″. (Also see color plate X.) (Sam Bruccoleri)

Here is a fine example of a Rhode Island continuous-arm chair with vigorous turnings and long leg taper. The influence of the New York City style is evident in the arm supports, basic leg turning pattern, spindles, and double ringing on the medial stretcher. In contrast, the spindles have narrower bases than New York City Windsors, the seat rolls up more from the underside than the seats of New York chairs, the top baluster of the leg is different, and, of course, the concave leg taper is quite different. The painted surface of this chair is wonderful.

161

161.   Armchair. Rhode Island, 1785–1800. Branded P. N. W. One of a pair. Very early black paint over the original green. Crest rail and spindles, hickory; arm supports, legs, and stretchers, maple; seat, pine. SW 16¾″, SD 17″, SH 17″, OH 36½″. (Joan and Don Mayoras)

Compared with figure 160, this is a less successful example of a Rhode Island version of a New York continuous-arm chair. The leg turnings are much more Rhode Island in style—in the reel and baluster, for example, and in the very distinctive drooped collar just below the first baluster. The baluster terminations of the medial stretcher also are a Rhode Island feature. Note that all the spindles of this chair pierce the bow. Like figure 160, this chair has a very fine early black paint surface over the original green.

However, although this is a fine chair, it is not quite equal to figure 160. The turnings are a bit heavy in the legs, stretchers, and arm supports; and lack the wonderful extremes of narrow-to-bulbous that make figure 160 so elegant.

ROD-BACK

~

CHAIRS

First introduced in Philadelphia around 1800, the rod-back, or Federal, Windsor style seems to have been an immediate success. The style quickly spread to most chairmaking centers from Maryland to Maine, New York being one of the notable exceptions.

Earlier Windsors had been used in outdoor settings, but the rod-back achieved a full *integration* with such settings. With its trellis-like back and turning patterns simulating bamboo, the rod-back has the organic feeling of a garden. Quiet, simple, and frequently elegant, its style is one that I find generally delightful.

Often, the merits of the style have been judged in relation to earlier styles, such as the comb-back and the fan-back. In the past, I myself have been guilty of this. But there is no more value in such comparisons than in comparing a painter such as John Kensett with John Constable, or Winslow Homer with Charles Willson Peale. Different times pose different problems that result in new design solutions and expressions.

In the rod-back, I believe the Windsor chairmaker was finally able to unify all the various parts of the chair into a totality of design. In the past, the legs, stretchers, arm supports, and back posts were baluster-turned—a design holdover from the earlier William and Mary period. The parts of the chair were used in concert but never fused into a design whole. For the most part, turning patterns remained decorative.

With the bamboo rod-back pattern, introduced from England via the Orient, all the parts of the chair could be turned to resemble bamboo in various stages of growth—thicker for the legs, back posts, and crest rails, and thinner for the stretchers and spindles. The result was a unity and purity of design that had never before been achieved in a Windsor.

162

162. Armchair. Philadelphia, 1800–1820. Nineteenth-century cadmium yellow paint with black striping over the original pale yellow paint. Crest rails and back posts, oak; crest medallion and seat, poplar; spindles, hickory; arms, arm supports, legs, and stretchers, maple. SW 19½″, SD 16½″, SH 18″, OH 33¼″. (Also see color plate VI.) (Mr. and Mrs. Paul Flack)

A typical Philadelphia rod-back Windsor of its period with a so-called butterfly medallion in its back, this chair has the characteristic rolled-shoulder turning pattern at the bottoms of the back posts, at the tops and bottoms of the arm supports, and at the tops of the legs. Note the triple ringing on the bamboo-turned tenoned arms. One might expect the maker to have socketed the arms into the back posts at the middle bamboo rings, but instead the arms are socketed above, at the centers of the back posts.

Usually, several back spindles of these chairs penetrate the lower crest rail and are socketed into the upper crest rail—giving the back a "bird-cage" effect—but here that is not the case.

164. Armchair. Philadelphia, 1800–1820. Branded I. [John] CHAP-MAN. Old shellac finish. Crest rail, spindles, and back posts, hickory; arms, mahogany; arm supports, legs, and stretchers, maple; seat, poplar. SW 18½″, SD 16½″, SH 16¾″, OH 36½″. (Independence National Historical Park)

This handsome rod-back has only a single crest rail. The arms, which form a nice cyma curve, are tenoned into the back posts just like the arms of bow-back armchairs. Thus the chair exhibits features of both periods.

163. Armchair. Philadelphia, 1800–1830. Late nineteenth-century putty-colored paint over the original green. Crest rails and spindles, hickory; crest medallion, pine; back posts, arms, arm supports, legs, and stretchers, maple; seat, poplar. SW 18″, SD 16½″, SH 18¼″, OH 35¼″. (Eugene Pettinelli)

The top crest rail and arms of this Philadelphia rod-back have been joined in the so-called duckbill pattern to resemble mitered corners. Actually, the "mitered" joints are an illusion created by extensions at the ends of the crest rail and arms. Note the double beading on the front edge of the seat.

165. Side chair. Exeter, New Hampshire, 1800–1820. Branded G. L. ILSLEY/EXETER N.H. (Elizabeth R. Daniel)

There are interesting regional differences between this "butterfly bird-cage" Windsor and figure 162. First, the edge of the seat in figure 162 rolls down, whereas here the seat has a fairly sharp, beaded edge as well as "rain-gutter" beading on top that is typical of the New England style. Also, in the leg-turning pattern of figure 162, the thickest part of the leg is just below the seat, and the leg gradually narrows toward the foot; here, the leg is narrowest at the seat and widest at the foot. Note, too, that the bamboo turnings of figure 162 are concave between the ringing, while those of this chair are convex.

The backs of these chairs are sometimes steam-bent to create an arched back. This occurs more often on New England chairs than on those from Philadelphia. And, of course, on this chair the second spindle on each side penetrates the lower crest rail and frames the butterfly medallion.

If this chair were not branded, it could as easily be attributed to Connecticut or Massachusetts as New Hampshire. Not having developed an indigenous Windsor style of their own, New Hampshire craftsmen seem to have been most influenced by Massachusetts and Connecticut Windsors.

166

165

166. Armchair. Pennsylvania, 1800–1820. Original black paint with gilt striping. Crest rail, back posts, and spindles, hickory; medallion, pine; arms, arm supports, legs, and stretchers, maple; seat, poplar. SW 21½″, SD 20″, OH 59¼″. (The Metropolitan Museum of Art; gift of Hazel Kirk Koepler and Virginia Lee Koepler, in memory of Olivia Hamilton Verne, 1975)

This remarkable ceremonial chair has a square pine insert in the top of its back on which is painted the Masonic symbol. The spindles are very well articulated. The arms are beautifully carved, with good knuckle terminations—a rare feature on rod-back Windsors. The piece is probably one of a kind.

167. Armchair. Connecticut, 1800–1820. Medial stretcher missing. Old red paint over black, over the original green. Crest rails, spindles, back posts, and arm supports, hickory; arms, legs, and stretchers, maple; seat, poplar. SW 20½″, SD 17¼″, SH 18¾″, OH 43½″. (Mr. and Mrs. R. W. P. Allen)

Here is a very lovely but eccentric rod-back armchair. The back is beautifully realized: the distance between the first and second crest rails is especially effective and dramatic, emphasizing the four penetrating spindles. The graceful cyma curve of the arms echoes the arm style of earlier tenon-arm, bow-back Windsors such as figure 138, and the handholds are well scrolled. Note the interesting overlapping or stepped-down turning pattern of the arm supports, which is repeated on both crest rails. The seat is nicely carved, with sharp corners reminiscent of the shield-shaped seats of Hepplewhite-style formal chairs. The leg turnings are of the double-ringed bamboo type often found on Connecticut Windsors.

168

167

168. Armchair. Connecticut, 1800–1820. Nineteenth-century dark brown paint over the original green. Crest rail, back posts, arms, arm supports, and legs, maple; spindles and side stretchers, hickory; seat, pine. SW 17⅛″, SD 17″, SH 18″, OH 38⅛″. (Nancy and Tom Tafuri)

Once again we see a chair that exemplifies the creativity of Connecticut Windsor-makers and their ability to spice up a potentially mundane product. The bamboo leg turnings of this chair are generally similar to those of figure 167, but they also have the feeling of tapered baluster-turned legs. The bamboo scoring is deeper than normal, and midway between the scoring is an unusual ring. The arms, arm supports, and medial stretcher precisely echo the shape of the legs, but the back posts and crest rail make only a vague attempt at it. The back posts end in nipple-like finials, and, oddly, the spindles have no bamboo scoring. The shield-shaped seat, normally found on Connecticut continuous-arm chairs, is unusual for a rod-back. Overall, this graceful chair creates an interesting visual experience.

169. Side chair. Pennsylvania, probably Bucks County or Chester County; 1790–1810. Probably cut down about 1½". One of a pair. Nineteenth-century dark green paint, with orange spindles and stretchers, over the original white paint. Crest rail and back posts, oak; spindles, hickory; seat, pine; legs and stretchers, maple. (Howard Szmolko)

This is an example of the Philadelphia-style "Sheraton" rod-backs that were produced in Philadelphia and nearby counties. Such chairs usually have seats that are better articulated, and overall they can be much more sophisticated.

169

170

170. Side chair. Pennsylvania, possibly Easton area; 1790–1810. One of eight. Refinished; traces of green paint. Crest rail, spindles, back posts, legs, and stretchers, hickory; seat, pine. SD 14¾", SH 17", OH 36". (Downingtown Antiques)

Chairs such as this one are known to have come from the Easton, Pennsylvania, area. The extreme serpentine crest-rail shape is repeated on the front edge of the seat, and the double beading of the crest rail can be found on the front edge and sides of the seat. The spindles are very effective, with one bamboo score mark and then a long taper to the top of the chair. The bamboo legs are graceful, with a well-placed H-stretcher arrangement.

171.   Side chair. New Hampshire, 1800–1820. Branded J. R. HUNT.
(New Hampshire Historical Society)
        This simple rod-back clearly shows the false mitered corners
where the crest rail meets the back posts, a feature of many rod-backs.
The rather nondescript seat is not as nicely realized as the back.

171

172

172.   Side chair. Philadelphia, 1810–1825. One of a pair. Original
yellow paint with black striping. Crest rail, back posts, legs, and
stretchers, maple; spindles, hickory; seat, pine. SW 16⅛", SD 16¼",
SH 17¼", OH 34½". (Mr. and Mrs. Paul Flack)
        Some rod-backs have solid, flat crest rails, like this one. The
triple bamboo scoring, box stretcher, button back-post finials, and
cushionlike Hepplewhite-style seat shape are frequently found on
Pennsylvania rod-backs.

173.   Side chair. Philadelphia, 1810–1825. Traces of old white paint over the original red. Crest rail, oak; spindles, hickory; back posts, legs, and stretchers, maple; seat, poplar. (John Bartram Association)

Similar to figure 172 in nearly every respect, this chair has a more elaborate step-down crest rail.

174.   Side chair. Philadelphia, 1810–1830. Traces of the original white paint. Crest rail, back posts, legs, and stretchers, maple; spindles, hickory; seat, poplar. SW 16¼″, SD 15½″, SH 17½″, OH 33″. (John Bartram Association)

Although comparable to figures 172 and 173, this chair is somewhat later, as is evident from the seat design: a simple, squared-off plank with very little attempt at carving.

173

174

175

176

175. Armchair. Philadelphia, 1810–1830. Nineteenth-century mahoganized grain painting. Crest rail and back posts, maple; arm supports, seat, legs, and stretchers, poplar; spindles, hickory; arms, pine. (Independence National Historical Park)

This massive rod-back belonged to Bishop White of Philadelphia, the first American bishop consecrated by the Church of England and one of the two official chaplains of the Second Continental Congress. This chair has legs that fit into small wooden blocks with the same paint history as the rest of the chair. The purpose of these blocks is unknown.

176. Armchair. Massachusetts, probably Boston; 1820–1830. Original chocolate-brown paint decorated in yellow, red, green, and black with yellow striping. Crest rail, back posts, arm supports, legs, and stretchers, maple; spindles, hickory or white oak; arms, mahogany; seat, poplar. SW 19″, SD 19¼″, SH 17¾″, OH 48½″. (Collection of Melissa and Gary Lipton; courtesy of David A. Schorsch, Inc.)

Rod-backs with step-down crest rails were popular in New England at the beginning of the nineteenth century. Such chairs were produced around 1810, but the arms of this chair are its latest feature—more akin to those of the so-called Boston rocker of the 1825–1840 period. The comb-piece of this chair is simply a smaller version of the crest rail below it. The five supporting spindles of the comb-piece are socketed into the crest rail and are not extensions of the back spindles. This is a commode chair: the center section of the seat is hinged at the back and can be lifted.

177

176 A

176A. Armchair. Detail of crest, showing painted decoration.

177. Side chair. New England, probably Maine; 1810–1830. One of four. Original golden-yellow paint with red, black, and brown decoration. Crest rail and seat, pine; spindles, hickory; back posts, legs, and stretchers, maple. SW 15½″, SD 15″, SH 18¼″, OH 35″. (Claude and Alvan Bisnoff)

This chair may have been made by Windsor-maker and painter Daniel Stewart, who worked in Farmington, Maine, from 1812 to 1827, since it is remarkably similar in form and paint decoration to another chair which bears Stewart's label.[16]

178. Side chair. New England, 1815–1830. Original mustard-color paint with black decoration. Crest rail, back posts, legs, and stretchers, maple; spindles, beech; seat, pine. SW 15¾″, SD 16″, SH 17½″, OH 36″. (Marianne Clark)

A version of the step-down arrow-back Windsor, this chair has a rather ambitious crest rail that is carved up from the bottom to accentuate the top curve (unlike the previous two examples, which have crest rails with flat bottoms). The paint decoration is very elaborate, and the success of the crest rail's large rectangular panel depends upon its painted vine-and-fruit motif. From the seat down, the chair is a typical late New England rod-back design.

178

179

179. Armchair. Maryland, 1810–1830. Two coats of original brown paint. The entire chair is maple, except the poplar seat. SW 18¼″, SD 17″, SH 18½″, OH 35½″. (Also see color plate XIII.) (Charles Sterling)

The rolled knuckle arms of this chair are similar to those found on other chairs from Maryland, such as figures 127 and 127A. Otherwise, the chair is "normal" until we come to the crest rail, which is a tour de force. Actually, the crest rail is positioned like that of a fan-back chair. Its general contour is somewhat similar to the Lancaster County pattern, and the carving is highly individualized, with matchstick incised triangles flanking a central medallion, leaf patterns, and more matchstick incising on the ears. Note, too, that the matchstick carving is repeated at the tops of the handholds.

WRITING-ARM

CHAIRS

～

CHAPTER EIGHT

After having seen at least a hundred writing-arm Windsor chairs, I have observed that 60 to 70 percent of them were produced in Connecticut, and at least half of those were made by the E. B. Tracy shop. This conclusion is based on branded examples, woods used, construction methods, and turning patterns. Thus the form probably originated in Connecticut, perhaps with Tracy. However, no matter where writing-arm Windsors come from, they represent a rare form.

Almost no writing-arm chairs were produced in Philadelphia, with the exception of low-back versions made by Anthony Steel in the last decade of the eighteenth century; one Pennsylvania-style rod-back chair (branded ROSE) that I have seen; and a handful of writing-arm adaptations of "normal" Windsor armchairs. New York and Rhode Island also are notably lacking in examples of writing-arm Windsors. Massachusetts produced a few, but not many.

Basically, there are three ways to make them: from the ground up, as a unified, new design; as an adaptation of a normal Windsor, with a writing paddle substituted for the original arm; or with a writing paddle merely tacked on over the original arm.

The latter version usually is not particularly interesting, and perhaps it isn't really a writing-arm Windsor at all. The ground-up examples tend to be quite practical; they are usually more massive, with wider seats and extra space for drawers, candle slides, and the like. However, they are sometimes rather clumsy-looking because of their bulk. The writing-arm adaptations, on the other hand, are often quite graceful, especially the comb-backs.

180.   Writing-arm chair. Philadelphia, 1765–1780. Back legs pieced out about one inch. Refinished. Crest rail and arms, oak; spindles, hickory; writing paddle and seat, poplar; arm supports, legs, and stretchers, maple; wing nut, wrought iron. SW 25⅛″, SD 17″, SH 17⅜″, OH 44¾″, writing paddle 12¾″ × 23⅝″. (Privately owned)

Although this chair was originally pictured in *The Windsor Style In America*,[17] I can now provide information about its woods and dimensions. I now feel that this rare Philadelphia chair probably is a product of the same shop that made the low-back settee shown in figure 201; the turning patterns of the arm supports, legs, and stretchers are virtually identical.

181.   Writing-arm chair. Lisbon, Connecticut, 1780–1803. Branded EB: TRACY, with three hash marks under the seat and arm drawer. Black paint, over late nineteenth-century red, over yellow, over green. Crest rail and arms, maple; arm crest and writing paddle, pine; spindles, cross-braces, and stretchers, hickory; arm supports and legs, maple; seat, chestnut. SW 27⅛″, SD 18⅞″, SH 15¾″, OH 46⅞″, writing paddle 18¾″ × 26½″. (Steven and Helen Kellogg)

Considering the large number of Tracy writing-arm chairs that have turned up over the years, one could conclude that making such Windsors was a specialty of his. This is an excellent chair and a typical Tracy product in that it has one tongue and two supports to hold the writing tablet.

182.   Writing-arm chair. Connecticut, 1800–1810; descended in a
Burlington County, New Jersey, family. Nineteenth-century
mahoganizing, over straw-colored paint, over the original blue-gray
paint. Crest rail, arm crest, arms, and legs, maple; spindles, arm supports, and stretchers, hickory; seat and writing paddle, pine. SW
27⅛", SD 18", SH 17¼", OH 46¾", writing paddle 18¾" × 25¼".
(Privately owned; courtesy of the Burlington County Historical
Society)

    This is a fine example of a late writing-arm chair produced by
one of the Tracys. Stylistically and proportionally, the piece is simply
a bamboo-turned, toned-down expression of figure 181. Note, for
example, the similarities of the comb-pieces, the use of six tall back
spindles, the arms, arm crests, front edges of the seats, stretchers, and
the writing tablet construction—all unmistakable E. B. Tracy features
that are found on all branded Tracy comb-back writing-arm chairs.

182

183

183.   Writing-arm chair. Probably Lisbon, Connecticut; 1780–1803.
The gallery around the writing surface is a nineteenth-century addition. Mid-nineteenth-century black paint with gilt striping over the
original green paint. Arm crest, arms, arm supports, legs, and
stretchers, maple; spindles, ash; writing paddle, pine; candle slide
and drawer, chestnut; seat, possibly maple. SW 27¼", SD 19", SH
15½", OH 27", writing paddle 18¾" × 25½". (Steven and Helen
Kellogg)

    Because this chair is virtually identical to others that are
marked with the brand of Ebenezer Tracy, we can attribute it to him.
Like the others, this chair has one tongue and two writing tablet supports, and all the spindles penetrate the arm crest. The turnings are
just like those of figure 181, but the legs have a bit more taper. A
candle slide beneath the writing-arm drawer is always a welcome feature on a writing-arm chair.

184

184.   Writing-arm chair. New Bedford, Massachusetts, 1800–1825. Branded SWIFT (probably Reuben & William Swift). Early green paint over the original green. Crest rail, spindles, arms, and arm supports, hickory; writing paddle, legs, and stretchers, maple; seat, pine. SW 27″, SD 16⅝″, SH 18″, OH 38½″. (Steven and Helen Kellogg)
      Here we see early nineteenth-century double-bobbin turnings above the seat of this chair combined with earlier vase-and-ring turnings on the undercarriage. Indeed, the top of the chair is so simplified compared with the undercarriage that it suggests the maker was not terribly confident in his ability to make a writing-arm chair. Had he used vase-and-ring-turned arm supports, he would have had to turn them very precisely. Instead, he used a simple double-bobbin design, which allowed him to cut the arm supports any length he chose. In the photograph we can see that the three writing-arm supports, although turned similarly, are cut completely differently to compensate for the fact that they are three different lengths. Note also the leg turnings—typical of Rhode Island, but found in Massachusetts and Connecticut as well.

185.   Writing-arm chair. Connecticut, 1780–1800. Original black paint. SW 20″, SD 14″, SH 17″, OH 36¼″, writing paddle 18″ × 26″. (Privately owned)

This is a very interesting variant of the well-known Tracy type of Connecticut writing-arm chair. This chairmaker, unlike Tracy, used knuckle handholds, two tongues, and three writing tablet supports. Also, note that the front edge of the seat is chamfered, but there is no attempt at saddling. The back is quite short for a chair of this overall size.

185

186

186.   Writing-arm chair. Massachusetts, probably Concord; 1790–1820. Top writing paddle a later addition. Made in white pine, maple, and ash. SW 18″, SD 16⅜″, SH 16½″, OH 39¾″. (Concord Antiquarian Society)

According to the Concord Antiquarian Society, this chair was owned by the Rev. Ezra Ripley (1751–1841), who bequeathed it to his step-grandson, Ralph Waldo Emerson. It also was used by Nathaniel Hawthorne at the Old Manse between 1842 and 1845. The unusual leg turnings are nearly identical to those of figure 92. The original writing tablet is probably below the later addition, which was used to raise the height of the writing surface. The original writing arm probably had a drawer or candle slide. Like figure 185, this chair has an unusually short back.

187.   Writing-arm chair. Probably Connecticut, 1790–1810. Old black paint over traces of the original green. Crest rail, hickory; spindles, hickory or chestnut; arms, arm supports, legs, and stretchers, maple; writing paddle, poplar; seat, pine; drawer, poplar with cherry divider. SW 24¾″, SD 18⅜″, SH 16¾″, OH 43³⁄₁₆″, writing paddle 17³⁄₁₆″ × 24″. (Philip Bradley Antiques)

This is a provincial chair. The double score marks on the arm supports are found on many Connecticut Windsors, and the comb is very "Connecticut" in style. All told, this is a pleasing, quaint attempt at building a stylish writing-arm Windsor chair.

187

188

188.   Writing-arm chair. Richmond, Virginia, 1802. Dated label of Andrew and Robert McKim. Restored black paint with yellow decoration. Crest rail and back posts, oak; spindles, arms, and arm supports, hickory; writing tablet and seat, poplar; legs and stretchers, maple. SW 24⅜″, SD 17⅞″, SH 18″, OH 37⅞″, writing paddle 18⅞″ × 29³⁄₁₆″. (Museum of Early Southern Decorative Arts, Winston-Salem, N.C.)

This type of rod-back Windsor chair—with its squared-off, beaded crest rail—usually is the most successful of the rod-back designs. The maker of this chair paid great attention to details not usually found on rod-backs: the crest rail is nicely shaped; the beading on the arms continues onto the back posts; the back posts are bamboo-turned; the writing tablet is beaded; the handholds are scrolled; the legs are boldly turned with good splay; the medial stretcher is baluster-and-ring-turned; and there are nine spindles in the back and four under each arm. This chair is no doubt based on a Philadelphia model such as figure 164—right down to the rounded shoulders at the tops of the legs where they enter the seat—and it would be difficult to determine its origin if it were not labeled.

189.   Writing-arm chair. Philadelphia, 1800–1820. Nineteenth-century brownish-red paint, over straw-colored paint, over the original green. Crest rail, spindles, and arms, hickory; back posts, arm supports, and legs, maple; seat and writing paddle, pine; stretchers, hickory and poplar. SW 20¾", SD 16¼", SH 17¼", OH 35¼", writing paddle 17⅜" × 23¼". (Burlington County Historical Society)

Here we see what is basically a rod-back bird-cage armchair with a writing tablet added over the original arm. Since the writing tablet has the same paint history as the rest of the chair, it is not a later addition. The flat writing-tablet support dovetails into the writing tablet and the side of the seat.

Very few writing-arm chairs were made in Philadelphia, and even fewer as rod-backs. This chair is merely a late adaptation of a form that had waned in popularity.

189

190

190.   Writing-arm chair. New Jersey, 1800–1820. Branded A. THAYER. Drawer under writing paddle missing. Nineteenth-century dark brown paint, over blue-gray paint, over the original green. Arm crest and arms, hickory; spindles, arm supports, legs, and stretchers, maple; writing paddle and seat, pine. SW 24", SD 16¼", SH 18½", OH 33", writing paddle 16¼" × 23⅜". (Dowingtown Antiques)

Very few low-back writing-arm chairs have steam-bent (as opposed to sawed) arm rails, which makes this piece unusual. Constructed in this way, the arm rail is pleasingly slender. The box-stretcher arrangement indicates a late date for this very simple but rather elegant piece. Note that the legs are turned with triple, rather than double, bobbins.

191.   Writing-arm chair. Probably Southern, 1790–1810. (Museum of Early Southern Decorative Arts, Winston-Salem, N.C.)
This very simplified provincial interpretation of a writing-arm chair has an almost homemade look. The bamboo-turned arms are a nice touch.

192. Writing-arm chair. Connecticut, 1820–1840. Original yellow paint with green and red decoration. Crest rail, back posts, spindles, arms, and arm supports, maple; writing paddle, pine; seat, legs, and stretchers, chestnut. SW 23⅜″, SD 16¾″, SH 15½″, OH 31⅝″, writing paddle 18⅜″ × 27½″. (Steven and Helen Kellogg)

Although it is a late chair, this has a wonderful folk-art quality. Its earlier-style bamboo turnings contrast with the "latest" pattern in the arm supports and spindles. The front stretcher is interesting because it is flat on its face but full-round on its back.

As construction of Windsors became simpler, the paint decoration became more elaborate and important—in fact, the chairs were purposely designed to accommodate fancy painted surfaces that would highlight the architecture of the chairs. This particular piece has its original yellow paint with green floral decoration trimmed in red.

192

193.   Writing-arm chair. New England, 1800–1820. The drawer is a later addition. Black paint over traces of the original white. Crest rail, oak; back posts, spindles, legs, and stretchers, hickory; arm, writing paddle, and seat, pine; arm supports, hickory and maple. SW 32⅝″, SD 20½″, SH 17½″, OH 32½″, writing paddle 21½″ × 33″. (Bill Jennens)

        Both the writing tablet and the arm of this chair were originally upholstered in black pigskin. Rather than create a tongue to support the writing tablet, the maker simply increased the seat width, giving the chair the feeling of a loveseat. This proportion fits nicely with the overall boxiness of the back and allows the chair to have 13 spindles.

193

ROCKING

CHAIRS

CHAPTER NINE

Windsor rocking chairs were produced in all the chairmaking regions throughout the second half of the eighteenth century, although they were few and far between until the end of the century. By the early 1800s, Windsor rockers had become extremely popular; one notable example in New England was the tall-backed "Salem rocker." But by the 1840s, Windsor rockers had been displaced by "fancy" rocking chairs such as the famous "Boston rocker."

As a rule, Windsor rocking chairs have relatively high backs and are often comb-backs rather than, say, bow-backs or sack-backs. They are usually armchairs, but side chairs do turn up. Elaborate paint decoration with striping and floral motifs is quite common, perhaps because the chairs were viewed as leisure, rather than formal, furniture.

While I have tried to limit this chapter to pieces that were originally created as rocking chairs, as opposed to those whose rockers were added later, the first example shown seemed too interesting to ignore.

194. Rocking chair. Massachusetts, 1780–1800. Spring rockers marked "Shaker Patent." Mid-nineteenth-century, mustard-color grained paint over the original green paint. Crest rail and arms, oak; spindles, hickory; arm supports, legs, and stretchers, maple; seat, pine; rockers, steel springs. SW 20¼″, SD 15¾″, SH 19″, OH 37″. (Whistler Gallery, Inc.)

Here is one way to convert a Windsor chair to a rocking chair—by adding Shaker Patent rocking springs to a nice Massachusetts sackback in the Philadelphia style. The chair, of course, predates the rocking springs, but traces of the chair's last coat of mid-nineteenth-century, mustard-color paint is also on the springs, which gives us some idea of when the springs were added.

194A. Detail of Shaker Patent rocking springs.

195. Rocking chair. Probably Pennsylvania; 1800–1820.
Nineteenth-century brown paint with gilt striping. Crest rail, oak;
back posts, spindles, and side stretchers, hickory; seat, poplar; legs
and medial stretcher, maple; rockers, walnut. SW 17¾″, SD 15¾″,
SH 16″, OH 36″. (Privately owned)

　　This is a good example of a Windsor rocking chair with legs
purposely turned to accept rockers. The shape of the so-called
"cheese-cutter" rockers is like that found on rush-bottom chairs that
date from the middle to the end of the eighteenth century. The
rockers are mortised into the legs and held in place with pegs. The fact
that it has no arms makes this rocker uncommon.

195

196.　Rocking chair. Probably New Jersey; 1810–1830. Original black
paint with yellow decoration. Crest rail, possibly oak; spindles, arm
supports, legs, stretcher, and rockers, maple; arms, ash; seat, pine.
SW 20½″, SD 15¾″, SH 15″, OH 42¾″. (M. Finkel & Daughter)

　　For this chair, the rockers serve a dual purpose: as rockers and
as side stretchers. The medial stretcher is doweled into both rockers,
and the thickness of the rockers allows the legs to be socketed into
them as well. The design of the rockers is slightly later than the rocker
design of figure 195.

　　This chair was found in New Jersey and has the slim turnings
of certain other New Jersey Windsors.

196A. Detail of rocker and leg construction.

196 A

196

197.   Rocking chair. Boston, 1790–1800. The name "Sanborn" is marked in chalk on the seat bottom, possibly by chairmaker Reuben Sanborn. Painted black. Top crest rail, arms, arm supports, legs, and stretchers, maple; crest rail, oak; seat, pine; rockers, birch. SW 19½″, SD 16¼″, SH 14½″, OH 43½″. (Mr. and Mrs. Thomas Helm)

Although this chair is a Boston interpretation of a Philadelphia bow-back form, the comb-piece arrangement we see here is never found on Philadelphia Windsors.

197

198

198.   Rocking chair. New England, 1800–1815. Original olive-green paint with yellow decoration. Top crest rail, legs, and stretchers, maple; crest rail, spindles, and arm supports, ash; arms, mahogany; seat, drawer, and rockers, pine. SW 20″, SD 18½″, SH 13½″, OH 42″. (David A. Schorsch, Inc.)

The top crest rail of this rocker is attached in an unusual way that creates nine "bird-cage" bars in the back of the chair. Also interesting is the "knitting drawer" under the seat that pulls out from the side.

Note how the legs are chamfered at the bottom where the cheese-cutter rockers are socketed.

199.   Rocking chair. New England, possibly Connecticut or New Hampshire; 1820–1830. Original yellow paint with green-and-gilt sponge decoration. Crest rail, spindles, arms, arm supports, legs, stretchers, and rockers, maple; seat, pine. SW 17¾″, SD 17″, SH 17½″, OH 46⅜″. (Steven and Helen Kellogg)

For this chair, as for figure 196, the rockers also serve as side stretchers. This piece is very similar to rocking chairs of this type that were made by A. Wetherbee of New Ipswich, New Hampshire.

199

200.   Rocking chair. New England, 1830–1840. Original yellow paint
with red-and-black decoration. Crest rail, back posts, spindles, arm
supports, legs, and stretchers, maple; arms, mahogany; seat, pine;
rockers, chestnut. SW 19¼″, SD 18″, SH 14″, OH 42¼″. (Steven and
Helen Kellogg)

Later Windsor rockers like this one are difficult to regionalize.
By the 1830s, they were almost identical in woods, construction, and
paint—especially rockers from Connecticut, Massachusetts, and New
Hampshire. This type of rocking chair may have been the forerunner
of the so-called Boston rocker.

200

SETTEES

C H A P T E R   T E N

Most of the earliest American Windsor settees—those from the 1750–1770 period—were made in Philadelphia and were low-backs, judging from surviving examples. Around 1765 or so, some sack-back settees were produced, but they apparently were never as plentiful as the low-backs—interesting, I think, because sack-back Windsor chairs far outnumbered low-back chairs.

The basic construction of the Philadelphia low-back settee was the same as that used for low-back chairs. Of course, the settees are longer, but their length did not weaken the construction of the back. This was not the case with the sack-back and the later bow-back settees. The necessary length of the spindles may be in part responsible for the fact that not many sack-back benches have survived intact; and the fact that the backs of these settees were not particularly sturdy may, in turn, account for the fact that not many were produced in the first place.

Bow-back, tenon-arm settees seem to have been made in larger numbers than sack-backs. Certain other forms were attempted, such as the continuous-arm settee, the tenon-arm fan-back settee, the armless bow-back settee, and the rare triple-back settee. However, it was the rod-back form of Windsor bench of about 1800 that was produced in the greatest numbers as well as in the greatest variety of color, decoration, and back design. During the first quarter of the nineteenth century, rod-back settees were produced as part of sets, often consisting of six side chairs, two armchairs, and a settee, all similarly paint-decorated. During this period two-person settees, or loveseats, also were popular.

As was true of chairs, the designs of settees were most conservative in areas such as Philadelphia and Boston, and most individualistic in Connecticut, Rhode Island, New Hampshire, and areas remote from the design centers. Interestingly, it is very rare to find a settee made in New York.

201.   Settee. Philadelphia, 1765–1780. Nineteenth-century crackled varnish over traces of red-and-green paint. Crest rail and seat, poplar; spindles, hickory; arms and handholds, oak; arm supports, legs, and stretchers, maple. SW 80″, SD 22½″, SH 17½″, OH 29½″. (Privately owned)

This is a very strong example of a Philadelphia low-back settee of the period. The turnings are robust and bulbous, probably a holdover design from the earlier blunt-arrow style. The arm supports are not vase-tapered, as they are in comb-backs, and are reminiscent of the work of Francis Trumble. The flaring seat edge conforms with the flare of the knuckles. This is one of the earliest examples of a vase-and-ring-turned settee. The seat is constructed of two boards. (Although the seats of settees are almost always made of a single plank, occasionally a two-board construction is used.)

201

202

203

202. Settee. Philadelphia, 1765–1780. Old black paint over traces of the original green. Arm crest, chestnut; arms, possibly oak; spindles, hickory; seat, poplar; legs and stretchers, maple. SW 60¾″, SH 15½″, OH 29″. (Wayne Pratt)

Like figure 201, this piece has an early character, especially noticeable in the turnings of the arm supports. While both pieces have an overall height of 29″ or so, this piece has a seat height of 15½″, while figure 201's is 17½″; thus figure 201 has a more compressed design that could be considered better. Figure 201 also has more spindles in its back. On the other hand, this settee has a desirable feature that figure 201 lacks: ringed side stretchers. Thus the two pieces are quite similar expressions with some interesting differences.

203. Settee. Philadelphia, 1765–1790. Branded I. [John] LETCH-WORTH. Approximately one inch of foot lost. Shellac finish. Arm crest and seat, poplar; arms, oak; spindles, hickory; arm supports, legs, and stretchers, maple. SW 76″, SD 21″, SH 16¾″, OH 32″. (Independence National Historical Park)

This settee is slightly later than the previous two examples. Its later features include the vase taper where the arm support enters the seat and the general slimness of the turning patterns. Its overall height is three inches more than the previous two settees—and it would be even taller were some of the feet not missing. This settee also has a remarkable 48 spindles.

204. Settee. Lancaster County, Pennsylvania, 1760–1780. Very old black paint over the original green. Arm crest, probably maple; spindles and arms, hickory; seat, pine; arm supports, legs, and stretchers, maple. SW 75″, SD 18¼″, SH 18″, OH 30″. (Privately owned)

Lancaster County settees are rare, and were no doubt made in smaller quantities than those from Philadelphia. These pieces have several distinctive characteristics, among them: a steam-bent arm rail; knuckles made in three pieces (with the sides and bottoms attached to the arm rail); slightly bulbous spindles; blunt-arrow feet on the front legs, and tapered rear legs; score marks on the balusters of the arm supports and legs; and ring-and-arrow turnings on the medial stretchers.

Another special characteristic of this settee and others with steam-bent arm rails (as opposed to those with sawed arm rails, such as figures 205, 206, and 207) is that the arm crest does not wrap around the top of the arm rail, and its width more or less corresponds to the distance between the outer back legs.

204

205.

205.   Settee. Lancaster County, Pennsylvania, 1780–1800. Original blue-gray paint. Arm crest and seat, poplar; spindles and arms, hickory; handholds, walnut; arm supports, chestnut; legs and stretchers, maple. SW 77¾″, SD 23″, SH 18″, OH 31″. (Privately owned)

Here is another good example of a Lancaster County settee, though later than figure 204. Like figure 204, it has a steam-bent arm rail, three-piece knuckles, slightly bulbous spindles, and characteristic side stretchers. However, the legs of this bench are of the double-bobbin variety, with a flared foot at the front and a tapered foot in back. (This flared foot is often called a "goat foot" in the Pennsylvania Dutch country.) The design of this flared front foot, like that of figure 204, is a more elaborate design than that of the back foot. Even with the use of the later, simplified bamboo turnings, this provincial Windsor-maker created a powerful design.

206.   Settee. Pennsylvania or Maryland, 1790–1810. Original paint. Arm crest, oak; spindles and arms, hickory; arm supports, legs, and stretchers, maple; seat, poplar. SW 84″, SD 22″, SH 17″, OH 32″. (Tom Brown)

This settee has several Lancaster County characteristics: a steam-bent arm rail; arm supports turned in the Lancaster style; and three-piece knuckles. But the bamboo leg turnings, the almost barrel-shaped side stretchers, and the double-bobbin medial

stretcher are not in the Lancaster County style. They are, however, found on settees from Maryland near the Pennsylvania border.

Note the extreme overhang of the seat beyond the legs, and, because of it, how proportionately short the arm crest appears.

207.   Settee. Pennsylvania or Maryland, 1790–1810. Nineteenth-century brown varnish over a putty-color ground, over gray-green paint, over the original green paint. Arm crest, handholds, and seat, poplar; arm supports, spindles, legs, and stretchers, hickory; arms, oak. SW 85″, SD 23¾″, OH 32½″. (The Henry Francis du Pont Winterthur Museum)

Though it appears similar to figure 206, this settee has an arm crest that is constructed differently. The arm crest is not a single, solid piece of wood, but has been created by nailing three separate strips of wood to the front, top, and back of the steam-bent arm rail, creating the illusion of a single piece of wood. As with the previous three examples, the knuckles of this settee are made in three pieces.

There are also several stylistic parallels to figure 206: the long seat overhang; the relatively short crest rail; the barrel-shaped side stretchers; the double-bobbin medial stretchers; the leg turnings (although these have a longer taper); the arm-support turnings; and the general shape of the knuckles. Of course, the one obvious difference is that the spindles of this settee are baluster-turned, which adds a great deal of visual energy.

206

207

208.   Settee. Pennsylvania, 1765–1780. Nineteenth-century crackled varnish. Arms, arm supports, legs, and stretchers, maple; spindles, maple and hickory; seat, pine. SW 76″, SD 19″, SH 18″, OH 30″. (Privately owned)

This is one of three known settees by this maker. It has a very unusual, dynamic design, with all spindles baluster-turned and with a rare bell-shaped cap that is echoed in the leg turnings. Only the center spindle is perpendicular, the others being progressively angled until the last spindle is parallel to the arm support. The bold knuckles (done in the Lancaster County style with a protruding center knuckle), shield-shaped seat (flared at the front edges), and baluster-like turning in the leg cylinder where the stretcher is socketed (where the leg would normally be straight) all mark this piece and the two others like it as the product of a single shop. At least one low-back armchair in exactly the same style is also known (see figure 36).

Note the beading on the front edge of the arm crest, which emphasizes an uncommon design feature of this piece: the arm crest,

which in a Philadelphia low-back would overlap the arms, in this piece and the two other examples is actually cut from the same piece of wood—that is, there is a mortise-and-tenon joint rather than a lap joint. This is actually a stronger joint than those used on Philadelphia low-backs.

It is unusual for a settee to have a medial stretcher pattern like the one found here, which, in fact, is just like that found on certain Delaware Valley rush-bottom chairs. The side stretchers are in the English taste and in a pattern found among Philadelphia and Rhode Island Windsors.

The tall, turnip-like blunt-arrow foot adds a nice finish to the leg. Scribe marks on the underside of the seat of this piece mark the tentative leg-hole placement, but the holes were drilled elsewhere, suggesting that this may have been an experimental piece or a prototype.

208

209.   Settee. Pennsylvania, 1765–1780; found in New Market, Maryland. Nineteenth-century mahoganizing over the original green paint. Arm crest and seat, poplar; spindles, arms, handholds, arm supports, legs, and stretchers, maple. SW 81⅝″, SD 21¼″, OH 32″. (The Henry Francis du Pont Winterthur Museum)

Here is the second settee by the same hand as figure 208. The construction is identical, but the embellishments are different. The knuckles are better realized on this piece, with more flare in the Chippendale style. The spindle turning pattern is practically the same, but the baluster turning is better. Though the top half of the leg is like that of figure 208, from midleg down the bulging cylinder is longer and the flaring collar of figure 208 is replaced by the more traditional reel and ring. The foot is a ball with a long nipple. The medial stretchers are a type found on Lancaster County fan-back, sack-back, and bow-back Windsors.

Perhaps this piece is slightly later than figure 208 and the "final design" derived from the prototype.

209

210

211

210. Settee. Probably Lisbon, Connecticut, 1770–1803. Nineteenth-century black paint over red, over blue, over the original green. Arm supports and legs, maple; arms, spindles, and stretchers, oak; seat, chestnut. SW 81½″, SD 22¾″, SH 15¾″, OH 30⅛″. (Mr. and Mrs. Victor Johnson)

This piece is attributable to Ebenezer Tracy of Lisbon, Connecticut.[18] It is a most exuberant example of Connecticut furniture and shows Tracy at his best. The rake of the two inside legs is unusual and makes the settee look almost like two chairs. Tracy seems to have paid more attention to the base of the piece than to the top, and the large, waferlike rings on the stretchers mark the piece as special and undoubtedly a custom order.

211. Settee. Philadelphia, 1780–1800. Branded A[nthony]. STEEL. Old varnish over traces of gray paint. Arm crest and seat, poplar; spindles, hickory; arms, oak; arm supports, legs, and stretchers, chestnut. SW 78″, SD 20½″, SH 18″, OH 30½″. (Chalfant & Chalfant Antiques)

Something of a "transitional" piece, this settee has bamboo-turned legs but vase-and-ring-turned arm supports and baluster-shaped medial stretchers with bamboo scoring. Like many Philadelphia low-back settees of the bamboo period, this one does not have knuckles. It is a typically conservative expression of Philadelphia furniture-making.

212. Settee. Philadelphia, 1780–1800. Branded D[aniel]. CARTERET. Late nineteenth-century black paint over older blackish-green paint. Arm crest, arm supports, legs, and side stretchers, maple; spindles and medial stretchers, hickory; arms and handholds, oak; seat, pine. SW 77¾″, SD 21″, SH 17⅝″, OH 32″. (Bernard & S. Dean Levy, Inc.)

A similar expression to figure 211, this settee has vase-and-ring turnings and bamboo legs, yet retains the full knuckle. The better taper of the legs and the presence of knuckles sets this piece apart from the ordinary. However, it also has the more typical bamboo medial stretchers.

212

213. Settee. Philadelphia, 1780–1800. Original salmon-color paint with black decoration. Crest rail, oak; arm supports and spindles, hickory; arms, mahogany; seat, poplar; legs and stretchers, maple. SW 69⅝″, SD 23⅜″, SH 17⅝″, OH 38⅜″. (Claude and Alvan Bisnoff)

Tenon-arm construction of bow-back Windsors was very fashionable during this period, and this settee is much like the chairs of its period. The seat width and depth are unusually long in overhang and extension.

213A. Settee. Side view showing seat width.

214.   Settee. Possibly Virginia; 1780–1800. Early nineteenth-century ochre paint over the original gray. Crest rail and spindles, hickory; arm supports and stretchers, possibly hickory; seat, poplar; legs, maple. SW 83″, SD 21½″, SH 17⅝″, OH 37½″. (Museum of Early Southern Decorative Arts, Winston-Salem, N.C.)

Based on the Philadelphia model of the period, this settee has the same general appearance as figure 213 but is much more detailed and elaborate. The piece is vase-and-ring turned throughout, and the arms are finely detailed, with beautiful knuckles. There are five sets of legs. The arms are mortised into the bow at a higher point than one would expect, making for a nice, flowing transition from bow to arm.

214

215

215.   Settee. New England, possibly New Hampshire; 1790–1800. Original dark red paint. Crest rail, oak; seat, pine; spindles, legs, and stretchers, hickory or chestnut. SW 48¾″, SH 17¼″, OH 36″. (Frank and Barbara Pollack)

A very rare form with no arms, this piece could almost be called a double-seat side chair. The bow is nicely pinched, and the form possesses a quiet elegance of design.

216.   Settee. Philadelphia, 1800–1810. Mid-nineteenth-century red grained paint, over a buff-color ground, over the original green paint. Crest rail, back posts, and spindles, hickory; arms, arm supports, legs, and stretchers, maple; seat, pine. SW 77¼″, SD 20⅜″, SH 17¼″, OH 34″. (Dietrich American Foundation)

Settees such as this are sometimes called "duckbill" Windsors. This is a newer, stylish design not based on the earlier vase-and-ring style. It is in pieces like this that the bamboo style, with its interesting angles, works best. The center post adds a nice symmetry and strength.

217.   Settee. Lancaster County, Pennsylvania, 1800–1820. Old dark brown paint over yellow paint, over the original salmon-colored paint. Crest rail, back posts, spindles, arm supports, and stretchers, hickory; crest medallions and seat, poplar; arms and legs, maple. SW 78¼″, SD 18⅝″, SH 16¼″, OH 33½″. (Downingtown Antiques)

A variation on the bamboo theme of figure 216, this piece is intended to give the illusion of three chairs side by side. The crest rail steps up distinctively to help create this effect, and the stretcher arrangement echoes that movement. This is a good example of a late settee, and was intended to be a companion piece to the so-called butterfly rod-back Windsor chairs of the period.

216

217

218

218. Settee. New England, possibly New Hampshire; 1790–1810. Original dark green paint. Made entirely in chestnut, except the pine seat. SW 66¼″, SD 16″, SH 17⅜″, OH 34″. (Privately owned)

Its curved seat, with its back, arms, and medial stretchers curved to conform to it, make this a very rare form. Interestingly, the medial stretchers are square in cross-section and are attached to the underside of the side stretchers with nails. All the spindles penetrate the crest rail and are wedged. The edge of the seat is beautifully carved with a concave chamfer, and the duckbill edges of the arms are nicely perked up.

219.   Settee. New England, possibly New Hampshire; 1790–1810.
Mid-nineteenth-century dark green paint over green paint, over the
original dark red paint. Crest rail, arms, arm supports, legs, and
medial stretchers, chestnut; spindles, hickory; seat, pine; side
stretchers, maple. SW 66¼″, SD 16¼″, SH 17½″, OH 35″. (Dietrich
Americana Foundation)
        This settee was probably made by the same hand as figure 218,
but here there is more overhang at the seat edge and an extra spindle
in the back.

219

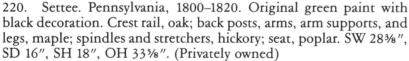

220. Settee. Pennsylvania, 1800–1820. Original green paint with black decoration. Crest rail, oak; back posts, arms, arm supports, and legs, maple; spindles and stretchers, hickory; seat, poplar. SW 28⅜″, SD 16″, SH 18″, OH 33⅝″. (Privately owned)

Small loveseats such as this are rare. This one has typical bamboo turning and is well proportioned. The ends of the seat are carved to simulate upholstery. The middle spindle and the third from each end penetrate the crest rail and are wedged.

221. Settee. Probably Pennsylvania; 1800–1820. Dark green paint over the original green. Crest rail and seat, poplar; back posts, arms, and arm supports, maple; spindles, legs, and stretchers, hickory. SW 31½″, SD 15″, SH 17½″, OH 34⅜″. (Privately owned)

Although made in the rod-back style, this settee retains the earlier H-stretcher pattern and baluster-turned side stretchers. The legs are double-bobbin turned. The three sets of legs and extra back post, plus the extra blocking on the front edge of the seat to echo the crest rail, make for a pleasing design.

222. Settee. New England, 1800–1820. Original yellow paint with black decoration. Crest rail and seat, pine; back posts, spindles, arms, arm supports, legs, and stretchers, hickory. SW 78″, SD 17″, SH 18½″, OH 37″. (Nancy and Tom Tafuri)

The design of this settee is like three chairs side by side, a design brought off successfully except for the problem of the center back post. (Perhaps, instead, the maker should have placed two back posts above the inner legs.) The crest rail is nicely carved and outlined in original paint decoration.

223. Settee. New England, possibly Maine; 1830–1840. Original yellow paint with green decoration. Made entirely in maple, except the pine seat. SW 78¼″, SD 18½″, SH 18½″, OH 34″. (Steven and Helen Kellogg)

I think that pieces like this could be called "family settees." This has the look of a Hitchcock chair and the arms of a Boston rocker.

The paint decoration, added both in freehand and in a plum-and-grape-leaf stencil pattern, creates most of the design interest and is even more important than the architecture of the piece.

222

223

224. Settee. Philadelphia, 1815–1840. Late nineteenth-century dark brown paint over traces of original stencil decoration. Crest rail, possibly poplar; back posts, spindles, arm supports, legs, and stretchers, maple; arms, oak; seat, poplar. SD 20¾″, SH 16½″, OH 32¼″. (John Bartram Association)

The bamboo spindles of late Philadelphia and other Pennsylvania pieces do not taper. Of course, they are easier to turn that way. This is a feature that is fairly consistent on chairs and settees with three-ring bamboo turnings. On this piece we see a simple board splat with arrow-shaped spindles. The ringing on the back posts gives a slight nod of acknowledgement to the earlier turning patterns. Pieces like this are often called "thumb-backs" because of the flattened terminal of the back posts.

224

CHILDREN'S
and
SCALED-DOWN
Furniture

The success of a small chair, high chair, or cradle has much to do with the attention to detail of the maker. When a small chair exhibits the same refinements one hopes to find on a full-size chair—such as knuckle handholds, carved ears, and excellent turnings—it not only says much about the chairmaker but also about the parents!

After all, a child's furniture needs are rather basic, sturdiness being the most important criterion. Parents who were willing and able to pay the extra price for the same refinements they enjoyed in their own Windsor furniture showed not only an appreciation for the Windsor form but an obvious love for their child. I think, too, that one can sense in child-size furniture a delight on the part of the chairmaker.

Fine children's Windsors are rare, not because they did not survive the rigors of childhood but because few were produced in the first place by practical craftsmen on a day-to-day basis. The better pieces were certainly special orders, and it took a truly fine craftsman to understand the problems involved in scaling down a normal chair to child's size. If all the parts are simply made proportionally smaller, the piece will look flimsy (and probably will *be* flimsy). The best Windsor-makers knew that parts such as arm supports and legs often should be made slightly heavier than one might expect to achieve the proper balance and proportion.

---

225. High chair. Philadelphia, 1765–1790. Branded I. [Joseph] HENZEY. Bottoms of knuckles missing; footrest an early replacement. Refinished; traces of original blackish-green paint. Crest rail, arm supports, legs, stretchers, and footrest, maple; spindles and arms, hickory; seat, poplar. SW 14⅞″, SD 10½″, SH 21⅝″, OH 37¾″. (Bernard & S. Dean Levy, Inc.)

Although this is a relatively late chair, it still retains the D-shaped seat of the earlier comb-backs instead of the expected oval or shield-shaped seat. An extra baluster has been added in the leg turnings to accommodate the dowel that holds the footrest; this extra baluster is repeated on the rear legs.

226. High chair. Philadelphia, 1775–1790. Branded I. [John] B. ACKLEY. Footrest an old replacement. Refinished; traces of the original green paint. Crest rail and arms, oak; spindles, hickory; arm supports, legs, and stretchers, maple; seat, poplar. SW 15″, SD 10¼″, SH 21¾″, OH 37¼″. (Mr. and Mrs. R. W. P. Allen)

Like figure 225, this chair has an extra baluster on the front legs, but the design is not repeated on the rear legs. Once again a D-shaped seat has been used. Holes in the arm supports for the missing restraining rod are clearly visible in the photograph.

Since the medial stretcher of this chair is original and in a late style—that is, it does not have turned rings at either end—the chair probably dates from closer to 1790 than to 1775.

225

226

227

227.   High chair. Philadelphia, 1780–1800. Footrest an early replacement. Nineteenth-century putty-color paint over the original dark gray paint. Crest rail, oak; spindles, hickory; arms and arm supports, mahogany; seat, poplar; legs and stretchers, maple. SW 14¼″, SD 14″, SH 21¾″, OH 36″. (Privately owned)

Here is a particularly handsome design. The mahogany arms and arm supports are an unusual touch. Note, too, that the arm supports are vase-and-ring turned, while the rest of the chair is bamboo-turned. The legs are turned in the typical Philadelphia style, with rounded shoulders at the tops of the legs. The seat is well saddled. On Philadelphia bow-backs of this type, a bamboo-turned medial stretcher is often found in combination with baluster-turned side stretchers.

228. High chair. Philadelphia, 1780–1800. Remnants of the label of Gilbert and Robert Gaw. Medial stretcher replaced. Original green paint over a salmon-color ground. Crest rail, oak; spindles, hickory; arms, mahogany; arm supports, legs, and stretchers, maple; seat, poplar. SW 14½″, SD 11⅝″, SH 20¾″, OH 36¾″. (Mr. and Mrs. Thomas Helm)

The leg turnings of this chair are somewhat better than those of figure 227, and the footrest is original, but from the seat up this chair doesn't quite match the sophistication of figure 227. The seat is not as well saddled, nor is it as deep from front to back. The arms are mahogany, but the arm supports are the more typical bamboo style of the period. There is only one short spindle under each arm of this chair, as opposed to two in figure 227—made possible by that chair's greater seat depth. This chair also has a "stiffer" back, with no pinch to the waist. Finally, the spindles are not as well turned—that is, they are essentially a straight taper with score marks and no articulation of the bamboo turning. The replaced medial stretcher of this chair no doubt originally looked like that of figure 227.

229. High chair. Philadelphia area, 1780–1810. Old dark red paint. Crest rail and arms, oak; spindles, hickory; arm supports, legs, and stretchers, maple; seat, poplar; footrest, pine. SW 14¼″, SD 10¾″, SH 20⅜″, OH 35″. (Mr. and Mrs. R. W. P. Allen)

The leg turning pattern of this chair, an interesting variant of the bamboo style, is occasionally found on Philadelphia chairs of this period. Overall, the chair is a fairly simple sack-back design. But it is unusual to find a sack-back, an earlier style, with these later bamboo turnings—the type one would expect to find on a tenon-arm, bow-back Windsor. Thus this chair may be provincial, perhaps from Chester County or Lancaster County. The heavy bamboo score marks and the baluster, rather than bamboo, medial stretcher also suggest a provincial origin.

228

229

230. High chair. New York City, 1770–1800. Refinished; traces of the original green paint. Crest rail, oak; spindles, hickory; arms, arm supports, legs, stretchers, and footrest, maple; seat, pine. SW 13⅜", SD 13½", SH 21¼", OH 35". (Privately owned)

Here we see one of the truly great examples of a Windsor high chair, with superb proportions and a wonderful splay. Note the innovative footrest: a baluster stretcher turning that is flattened on the top and bottom. New York—and New England—Windsor makers solved the problem of where to place the footrest by using a long leg taper and skortened baluster, so that the footrest could be socketed directly into the baluster. The H-stretchers on these chairs are also generally higher, and thus more graceful, than those on Philadelphia-area high chairs, whose footrests are generally socketed into the narrow part of the upper leg, weakening the leg. Occasionally, Philadelphia Windsor makers solved this problem by adding an extra baluster (as in figures 225 and 226) to receive the footrest instead of a longer bottom taper, but the result is awkward.

230

231. High chair. Salem, Massachusetts, 1800–1810. Branded I.C. TUTTLE. Early nineteenth-century yellow paint with white decoration over original green paint. Crest rail and arms, hickory or oak; spindles, hickory; arm supports, legs, and stretchers, maple; seat, pine. SW 15¾", SD 10¾", SH 21", OH 34". (Also see color plate VII.) (Doris and Kyle Fuller)

This is a fairly simplified version of a sack-back. On Philadelphia chairs the bamboo ringing is far more rounded, or convex, than it is on this chair, which is typical of the New England style. While most of this chair is bamboo-turned, the stretchers are baluster-turned—a feature not found on Windsors produced in design centers such as Boston.

The bow angles backward nicely, and the simplicity of the chair's design is enhanced greatly by its paint surface.

232

231

232. High chair. Gettysburg, Pennsylvania, or nearby Maryland, 1790–1810. SW 20⅞", SD 17½", OH 34⅝". (The Henry Francis du Pont Winterthur Museum)

This is an interesting variation on the high-chair form, with its great leg splay and graceful but idiosyncratic presence. The point where the arm sockets into the bow is lower than the point where the arm is attached to the arm support—just the opposite of most bow-back Windsor armchairs.

The turning pattern of the arm supports of this chair, especially as they enter the seat, is similar to that of figure 36, an armchair from the same area.[19]

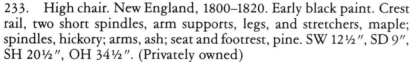

233

234

233. High chair. New England, 1800–1820. Early black paint. Crest rail, two short spindles, arm supports, legs, and stretchers, maple; spindles, hickory; arms, ash; seat and footrest, pine. SW 12½″, SD 9″, SH 20½″, OH 34½″. (Privately owned)

It is not unusual to find a New England comb-back with bamboo turnings, as on this simple, elegant little chair. The bamboo ringing has been placed toward the upper half of the legs, allowing for a long leg taper. Generally, three bamboo rings were used on rod-backs, so even though this chair has a comb-back form, it probably dates from no earlier than 1800.

234. High chair. New England, possibly New Hampshire; 1800–1820. Old dark brown paint. Made entirely in birch, except the pine seat. (Privately owned)

The attractive features of this "duck-bill" Windsor include its high back, the finely mortised corners of the arms and of the crest rail with its little ears, and the D-shaped seat. Perhaps the stretchers could have been placed higher, but the stretchers and legs are well turned, and the chair has good splay.

236. Armchair. Massachusetts, 1770–1790. Very old black paint over older black. Crest rail, oak; spindles, hickory; arms, arm supports, legs, and stretchers, maple; seat, pine. SW 14″, SD 13″, SH 10″, OH 32″. (Tom Brown)

This is a wonderful, charming example of a child's comb-back Windsor chair with all the refinements one would hope to find: scrolled ears, a tall back, knuckle handholds, a nicely saddled and chamfered seat, and crisp turnings.

When turning patterns are scaled down, it sometimes becomes difficult to determine where they were made. However, on this chair the arm supports and medial stretcher are just like those found on fan-back armchairs from coastal Massachusetts.

235

235. High chair. New England, 1800–1820. Nineteenth-century dark red paint over the original yellow. Crest rail, back posts, and legs, maple; spindles and stretchers, hickory; arms and arm supports, oak; seat, pine. SW 12¾″, SD 12″, SH 23½″, OH 36¾″. (Lori and Craig Mayor)

This rod-back high chair has an interesting feature: the back posts are round, with bamboo ringing, but they flatten when they reach the crest rail to conform with its shape. Unlike the arms of figure 234, these arms are totally different from the crest rail. The bamboo legs are nicely proportioned. The box stretcher arrangement is the one usually found on rod-backs.

236

237.   Armchair. New York City, 1775–1800. Old black paint over the original green. Crest rail, probably oak; spindles, hickory; arm supports, legs, and stretchers, maple; seat, poplar. SW 12½″, SD 12½″, tailpiece 2″, SH 12″, OH 25¼″. (Privately owned)

Here we see one of the masterpieces of children's Windsor furniture. It really leaves nothing to be desired and has all the refinements of the great New York City full-scale Windsors: explosive turnings and a strong shield-shaped seat, plus the added attraction of turned "pipe-stem" spindles that are probably a Rhode Island influence. Interestingly, except for a bit of heaviness in the spindles and legs, you would be hard-pressed to tell from this photograph the exact size of this little chair.

237

238.   Side chair. Philadelphia, 1765–1780. Some foot loss. Mid-nineteenth-century dark red paint over a salmon ground, over the original green paint. Crest rail, oak; back posts and spindles, hickory; seat, poplar; legs and stretchers, maple. SW 13¼″, SD 13¼″, SH 10¼″, OH 25¼″. (Privately owned)

A fine example of a scaled-down fan-back, this chair is not really as successful as figure 237. The stretchers are a bit clumsy compared with the leg turnings. The seat is well done.

Note how comb-pieces with uncarved ears like these usually turn up at the ends, whereas comb-pieces with scrolled ears turn down, as on figure 236.

238

239.   Armchair. Philadelphia, 1765–1790. Refinished; traces of green paint. Crest rail and arms, oak; spindles, hickory; arm supports, legs, and stretchers, maple; seat, poplar. SW 17¾″, SD 11¾″, SH 11″, OH 26¾″. (Mr. and Mrs. R. W. P. Allen)

The leg turnings of this chair are quite simple compared with those of figure 238, but the stretchers are much better and more in proportion to the legs. The arm supports are a bit simplified, the collar over the ring having been omitted. Overall, this is a nicely proportioned chair.

240.   Settee. Philadelphia area, 1790–1810. Refinished. Arm crest, poplar; spindles, hickory; arms, oak; arm supports, legs, and stretchers, maple; seat, poplar. SW 22¼″, SD 11½″, SH 8¾″, OH 17¼″. (Privately owned)

The arm crest on this low-back settee is nailed to the arm rail with original eighteenth-century nails. This settee never had stretchers. The leg turnings are extremely simplified, and it is quite possible that they were made by cutting down the tops of legs turned for a full-scale Windsor.

240

241.   Settee. Philadelphia, 1800–1830. Original red paint, with original salmon-color paint on seat. Crest rail, spindles, and stretchers, hickory; back posts, arms, arm supports, and legs, maple; seat, poplar. SW 36¾″, SH 12½″, OH 26¾″. (Sarah Lippincott)
     This is a very well-proportioned, scaled-down rod-back settee. The parts are nicely turned in the typical Philadelphia style. Especially attractive is the extra center back post, creating the illusion of a double chair.

241

242

243

242.   Side chair. Philadelphia, 1785–1800. Branded I. [John] B. ACKLEY. Rockers a later addition. Late nineteenth-century gray paint with green striping. Crest rail, probably oak; spindles, hickory; seat, poplar; legs and stretchers, maple. SW 14⅞″, SD 13¼″, SH 11¾″, OH 26¼″. (Eugene Pettinelli)

A child's version of the very popular Philadelphia bow-back side chair, this has the baluster side stretchers and bamboo medial stretcher characteristic of the form.

243. Armchair. New England, possibly New Hampshire; 1800–1820. Original black paint. Crest rail, spindles, back posts, arms, and arm supports, hickory; seat, pine; legs and stretchers, maple. SW 16½", SD 14½", SH 14", OH 30". (Courtesy, James and Nancy Glazer)

Very crisply turned for a bamboo child's chair, especially in the medial stretcher, this piece also has a beautifully chamfered seat that echoes the duckbill design of the arms and crest rail.

244

244. Armchair. Pennsylvania, 1800–1830. Painted black. Crest rail, back posts, arms, arm supports, and legs, maple; spindles and stretchers, hickory; seat, poplar. SW 11", SD 10¾", SH 6¾", OH 18½". (Privately owned)

This chair was originally made as a potty chair, and its scale is quite small. Yet even in this size, the legs have the typical Pennsylvania rolled shoulders at their tops where they enter the seat. The turned arms are similar to those found on rush-bottom, slat-back high chairs.

245.

245.   Armchair. Pennsylvania, 1800–1820. Original green paint with gilt striping. Crest rail, back posts, arms, arm supports, legs, and stretchers, maple; spindles, hickory; seat, pine. SW 4″, SD 3½″, SH 3½″, OH 7¼″. (See also color plate XV.) (Allan and Joan Lehner)

A true miniature only 7¼″ tall, this little chair could have been a doll's seat, a salesman's sample, or simply a whimsy. It is very well proportioned and an extremely rare piece of Windsor furniture.

OTHER FORMS
of
Windsor
Furniture

CHAPTER TWELVE

Tables, candlestands, and stools made with Windsor construction methods during the third quarter of the eighteenth century are very rare. This may have something do with the psychology of the Windsor-chairmaker of the time.

In the 1750s, it seemed innovative to transpose what were essentially William-and-Mary turning patterns to the new mode of seating furniture—the Windsor chair. However, "joyned" stools, tables, and candlestands had been produced with essentially those same turning patterns all through the late seventeenth and the first half of the eighteenth century. Thus, by the middle of the eighteenth century, while Windsor chairs looked new, tables and stools made with the same turning patterns must have seemed hopelessly old-fashioned.

It was not until the introduction of the bamboo turning pattern in the 1780s that the concept of a product totally Windsor in style but not a chair—the stool—seems to have been realized by Windsor craftsmen from all regions. By the end of the eighteenth century, stools of all shapes and sizes—from desk stools to "cricket" stools to work stools—were produced in large numbers.

In their leg turnings, these stools are usually stylistically similar to the bow-back or rod-back chairs produced in the same region. They also may display decorative beading on the edge of the top of the seat similar to the beading found on a chair's seat edge, and often they are painted in the variety of Windsor colors popular at the time.

Windsor tables and candlestands remained a great rarity, even in the bamboo period.

---

246. Candlestand. Philadelphia or Chester County, Pennsylvania, 1770–1800. Original black paint. Legs and stretchers, maple. Top 14½″ × 15¼″, OH 26¼″. (Dietrich American Foundation)

Windsor candlestands are rare, and ones that are in all-original condition, like this one, are extremely rare. This dish-top stand has sophisticated turnings in the Philadelphia pattern, but similar pieces have been found in Chester County, Pennsylvania. It is a delicate and graceful piece distinguished by a very long top baluster.

247. Table. Chester County, Pennsylvania, 1770–1800. Attributed to Nathan Jefferis (1773–1823), East Bradford Township. Made entirely in butternut. Top 16⅞″ × 17½″, OH 25″. (Chester County Historical Society)

It is not unusual for Windsor candlestands and tables to be constructed of a single wood, unlike Windsor chairs. The double beading on this table's dish top is an especially nice feature.

246

247

248

249

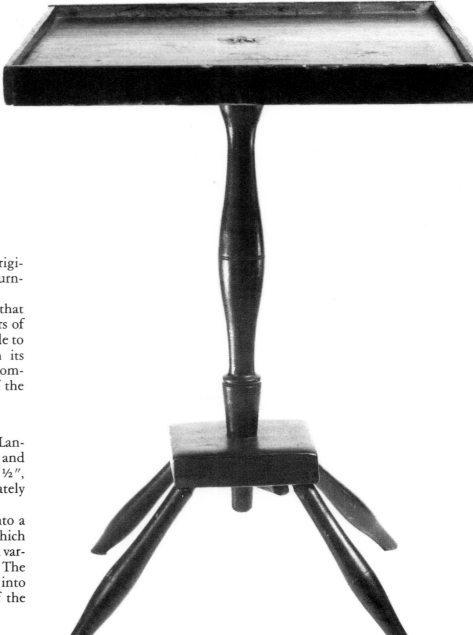

248. Stool. Pennsylvania, probably Philadelphia; 1780–1800. Original buff-color paint with yellow and green striping. Top, pine; turnings, poplar. Top 11″ × 11¼″, OH 27½″. (Privately owned)

This is a very unusual stool with a wonderfully turned top that shows clear evidence of concentric-circle chisel marks. Like chairs of the period, it has a top with a double banding along its edge made to resemble upholstery. Note the T-stretcher arrangement with its baluster-turned front stretcher and bamboo side stretchers—a combination of turning styles also found on Philadelphia chairs of the period.

249. Candlestand. Pennsylvania, probably Chester County or Lancaster County; 1750–1780. Original green paint. Top, pedestal, and cross-braces, poplar; plinth, pine; legs, oak. Top 17″ × 17½″, H to top of plinth 8¾″, OH 28″. (Also see color plate V.) (Privately owned)

While the previous forms have three legs that mortise into a circular top, this stand is constructed like a Windsor stool into which is socketed a center post with a top. Similar stands were made with various turning patterns throughout most of the eighteenth century. The top of this piece is held in place by a cross-brace that is mortised into the center post, and the center post is attached to the top of the "stool" with a removable wooden wedge, or key.

250. Candlestand. New England, 1800–1820. Nineteenth-century brown paint over the original green. Top and edge molding, pine; pedestal, maple; plinth, oak; legs, chestnut. Top 17¼″ × 17⅞″, OH 26″. (Rosemary Beck and Ed Rogers)

This is a more delicate version of figure 249. Each piece has decorative double score marks in the center of its pedestal and a shoulder at the bottom of the turning. The shape of the rectangular top is echoed by the top of the "stool," which in this case has four legs. The rectangular top is attached to the pedestal in typical Windsor fashion, with a wedge joint.

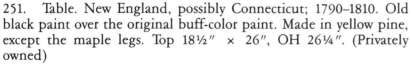

251.   Table. New England, possibly Connecticut; 1790–1810. Old black paint over the original buff-color paint. Made in yellow pine, except the maple legs. Top 18½″ × 26″, OH 26¼″. (Privately owned)

    Although this table does not have Windsor construction, but, rather, the more traditional frame construction, its leg turning pattern is nonetheless in the late Windsor style. More traditional splay-leg tables without stretchers have legs that are wide at the top and narrow as they approach the floor—no matter what the style of the leg. On this table, the legs are narrowly turned near the top, then swell at midleg, then taper to the floor—like the legs of figure 250. Note, too, the two decorative score marks on the legs, which are like the score marks on the pedestals of the two previous examples. The shape of the legs of this piece is reminiscent of the legs found on late Windsors made by E. B. Tracy, which also have double score marks.

252.   Stool. New England, 1780–1800. Nineteenth-century blackish-brown paint over the original green. Top, pine; legs and stretchers, maple. Top 9″ × 9½″, OH 10½″. (Privately owned)

    Stools like this are often called crickets, or hearth stools. This one has excellent proportions. Its thick, dished top above well-turned bamboo legs, plus its H-stretcher arrangement and baluster, make it one of the better stools of its type.

254. Stool. New York or eastern Connecticut, 1800–1810. Late nineteenth-century pewter-blue paint with gilt striping over pale gray paint, over white paint. Top, pine; legs and stretchers, maple. Top 9¾″ × 12⅞″, OH 9½″. (Mr. and Mrs. R. W. P. Allen)

Another cricket, this one bears a striking resemblance to a pair of footstools from the same period found on Long Island.[20] The cupid's-bow stretcher seen here is often found on Connecticut Windsor chairs. The box stretcher arrangement indicates a relatively late date.

254

253

253. Stool. New England, 1790–1810. Very old green paint over the original yellow. Top, pine; legs and stretchers, maple. Top 12³⁄₁₆″ × 12½″, OH 12¼″. (Privately owned)

Here is another well-proportioned stool. Especially effective is the high stretcher arrangement, allowing for a long leg taper—uncommon on a small stool.

256. Stool. American, 1790–1820. One replaced stretcher. Traces of white paint. Made entirely in oak. Seat 11″ × 11⅜″, OH 20″. (Privately owned)

This exceptionally sturdy stool apparently was made for heavy-duty use. One-quarter-inch-square pegs hold the legs to the seat and the stretchers to the legs. There are three score marks on the stretchers and legs—used not only for decoration but also to mark points of attachment.

256

255

255. Stool. New England, 1800–1820. Old yellow paint over traces of the original green. Seat, pine; legs and stretchers, maple. Seat 10¾″ × 13½″, OH 19¼″. (Mr. and Mrs. R. W. P. Allen)

Here is a tall stool with typical New England bamboo-turned legs. The high stretchers, long leg taper, and undercut chamfer of the top add a bit of grace to the piece.

257. Stool. American, 1800–1825. Late nineteenth-century brown paint with green-and-yellow striping over the original red paint. Seat, poplar; legs, maple; stretchers, possibly hickory. SW 12½″, SD 9″, OH 16¼″. (Mr. and Mrs. Victor Johnson)

Unlike most stools, this one has a chairlike seat. Because of its seat shape and leg arrangement, there is just one right way to sit on this stool—otherwise, it would tip over.

258. Stool. Pennsylvania, 1800–1820. Old gray paint over straw-color paint, over the original dark red. Seat, poplar; legs, maple; stretchers, hickory. Seat 13¾″ × 14″, OH 15½″. (Eugene Pettinelli)

With its staggered stretchers, this three-legged stool looks as though it were built for strength. The bamboo turning pattern is typical of Pennsylvania turnings in the rod-back period.

258

257

259.   Pair of stools. New England, 1800–1820. Original reddish-
brown paint with yellow ringing; original upholstery has been
replaced. Top, pine; legs and stretchers, maple. Top 9″ × 14″, OH
11½″. (Privately owned)
     The feature of these stools that raises them above the norm is
their leg turnings with a concave taper. Note how the maker chose to
use double score marks to accent the point at which the stretchers
enter the legs.

259

261. Table. Probably Pennsylvania; 1810–1830. Nineteenth-century stain over traces of the original green paint. Top, pine; legs and stretchers, poplar. Seat 11½″ × 20⅝″, OH 24⅜″. (Mr. and Mrs. R. W. P. Allen)

This is a very simple table, with bamboo-turned legs that socket into the top and are wedged.

261

260

260. Commode stool. New England, 1800–1830. Very old green paint with gilt striping over the original salmon-color paint. Frame, pine; legs, maple; stretchers, hickory. Seat 15¾″ × 16¼″, OH 12¾″. (Eugene Pettinelli)

The hole in the middle of this stool once held a slip seat. The top is framed with mortise-and-tenon joints, just like a slip-seat chair.

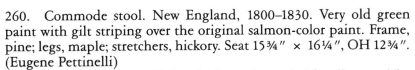

262.   Stool. New England, 1800–1820. Original mahoganizing over an ochre ground. Top, pine; legs, maple; stretchers, hickory. Top 10¾″ × 13¾″, OH 11¾″. (Privately owned)
   This stool is a rarity because it still has its original—or at least very early—needlepoint upholstery, edge-banded with silk ribbon.

262

263

263.   Stool. New England, 1800–1820. Traces of the original reddish-black paint. Seat, pine; legs and stretchers, maple. Seat 11″ × 11″, OH 18⅜″. (Privately owned)
   This stool looks rather like a New England Windsor chair, but, of course, there is no evidence that it ever had back spindles. Stools with definite "fronts," such as this one and figure 257, are uncommon.

264. Stool. New England, 1800–1820. Original dark red stain over salmon-color ground. Seat, pine; legs, maple; stretchers, hickory. Seat 13″ × 13¼″, OH 15½″. (Eugene Pettinelli)

The seat of this stool is carved to look like a cushion. It seems that stools became quite popular during the 1800–1840 period, judging by the frequency with which they are found in late styles with box stretchers.

265. Camp stool. Probably Pennsylvania, possibly Bucks County; 1800–1825. Reupholstered. Nineteenth-century dark red paint over black. Made entirely in maple, except for iron leg-joint pins. SW 17½″, SH 15½″, OH 30¾″. (Sam Bruccoleri)

Here is a novelty: a Windsor "director's chair" with double-bobbin legs and baluster-turned arm supports. Metal pins hold the legs together, and the legs are flattened at the point where they touch. Unlike modern director's chairs, this one cannot be completely folded.

264

265

266.   Daybed. New England, 1810–1830. (David Pottinger)
Windsor daybeds are rare. This one is made like a bow-back armchair, with a caned seat for comfort. The arrow-back spindles are nicely carved.

267.   Cradle. Vermont, 1810–1830. Branded D. HARVEY. Found in Passumsic, Vermont. Original salmon-color and black paint with black decoration. (Mr. and Mrs. Stephen Score)
Early Windsor cradles are relatively low to the ground, or they sit directly on their rockers, just like early board cradles. Later cradles, like this one, are much more chairlike and taller, perhaps because someone discovered that, since heat rises, an infant would stay warmer in a taller cradle. This particular piece has a plank bottom and a step-down crest rail just like a rod-back Windsor chair. The back posts are bamboo-turned and notched to accept the side rails.

This cradle has an odd feature: it rocks from front to back like a rocking chair, instead of from side to side. In this case, the rockers act as side stretchers.

The only difference between the headboard and footboard of this cradle is that the headboard steps down. The original paint decoration is quite attractive.

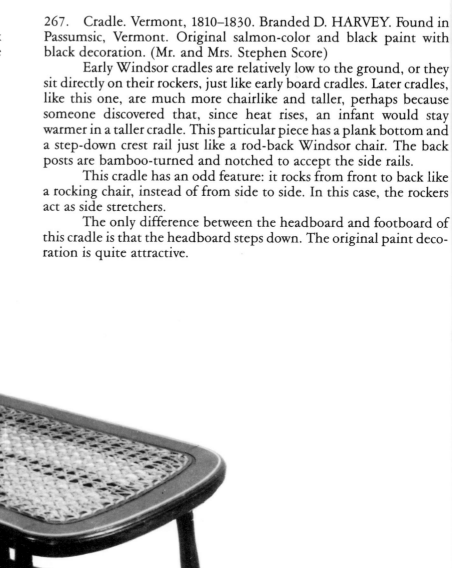

266

267

268

268.   Crib. New England, 1810–1830. Original red paint with yellow decoration. Crest rails, headposts and footposts, rails, spindles, legs, and stretchers, maple; bottom, pine. L 22½″, W 12¾″, H 15½″, OH 30″ (head) and 25½″ (foot). (Mr. and Mrs. Victor Johnson)

This "thumb-back" crib has split spindles instead of full-round turnings. It is unusual because it was made to be a crib and never had rockers. The casters seem to be original.

269.   Child-tender. New England, 1800–1830. Crest ring, seat, and drawer, pine; spindles, hickory; legs and stretchers, maple. SW 21¼″, SD 21⅜″, SH 12½″, OH 29¼″. (The Clokeys)

Here is a rarity: a Windsor child-tender. It is basically a large Windsor stool with a circular, cagelike arrangement of spindles. Because it is wide at the bottom and narrow at the top, it is virtually impossible for its small occupant to tip it over.

270.   Baby walker. New England, 1800–1830. Never painted; original casters; legs are probably shortened where casters worked their way loose and had to be refitted. Top, apron, and tray, pine; legs and stretchers, maple; casters, brass. Top 13¾″ square, tray 5″ × 13¾″ × 3″, OH 16″. (Mr. and Mrs. R. W. P. Allen)

This is certainly an unusual example of Windsor furniture. The small knob on the left side of the top of this piece, when turned, allows the top to open so a baby can be placed inside and practice walking while rolling around on the casters. Lest you think this is merely a cut-down Windsor chair fitted with an odd superstructure, look at the legs of this piece: they are turned with blocks at the top, as they would be for a table (or a baby walker!), but not for a chair.

269

270

Brands and Labels: The Maker's Mark

The practice of using printed paper labels to identify the makers of furniture was not common among early American craftsmen, although many case pieces, clock cases, and tables from the 1730s to 1830s retain their original paper labels.

A paper label provided an opportunity for a furniture-maker to create a small advertisement, sometimes listing his products, to accompany each piece produced in his shop. Because of climatic conditions, wood shrinkage, wood smoke, scratching, and peeling, most early paper labels haven't survived, or are in such poor condition as to be illegible, but I suspect that the biggest obstacle to the survival of paper labels is the glue or bonding material used to attach them to the wood. With the passage of time the glue becomes dry and brittle and loses its bonding properties, and the label falls off.

Many of these hazards were overcome on case pieces by the placement of the label: glued to the inside of the pendulum door of a tall case clock, or the outside of a small interior drawer of a slant-lid desk, or under the lid of a blanket box, or cellerette, a paper label is protected from the climate and the general wear and tear of everyday use. Fortunately, this has resulted in the identification of a considerable number of case pieces, clock cases, and other furniture products as the work of individual craftsmen in various regions of early America. Unfortunately, this usually is not the case when it comes to Windsors.

Because Windsors are all exterior, there are no protected places where a label can remain dry or reasonably secure for any length of time. The seat bottom is the only logical place for identification, since it presents the only unused Windsor surface. Nevertheless, that surface is exposed to climatic changes. Although some labeled Windsors have survived, it is difficult to determine to what extent labels were used. If a label was lost or removed in the first few years of a chair's existence, there would be no telltale rectangle of lighter-colored wood to show where the label was once attached.

Most Windsor-makers preferred to use the more permanent and practical method of branding their furniture—an identification not nearly as descriptive or elaborate as a label, but more enduring. Some chairmakers used both label and brand. Gilbert & Robert Gaw of Philadelphia, and Robert Taylor, also of Philadelphia, are examples of Windsor chairmakers whose branded chairs are often found, but whose chairs occasionally turn up with a label instead. I have seen a few chairs by other makers that were both labeled and branded (including one by William Seaver of Boston, illustrated in Appendix II).

By the third quarter of the eighteenth century, the business of exporting Windsors had expanded considerably, as ship captains found a lucrative Windsor market in seaports up and down the eastern seaboard. Often these vessels carried Windsor chairs from several chairmaking shops on the same voyage. On March 10, 1791, four dozen Windsor chairs were shipped to Petersburg, Virginia, on board the Schooner Thomas. The schooner's journal lists a payment of £12.00 to William Cox for two dozen, and a payment of £13.4.0 to Joseph Henzey for two dozen at £11/doz. Identifying the chairs from a particular shop was one very important way of keeping the inventoried cargo in agreement with the ship's manifest. Since loss and damage caused by salt water and dampness were a part of sea shipment at that time, it is not hard to see why Windsor chairmakers preferred branding to paper labels in order to avoid the confusion that could result from peeling labels.

The products of many of the Windsor chairmaking shops were so similar—especially the comb-back, sack-back, and bow-back styles popular during that period—that the method of branding quickly became the most common and practical way to mark a chair for export.

A Checklist of Windsor-Makers

This checklist, while admittedly far from complete, should nevertheless be of great help to owners of Windsor furniture in identifying provenance. Many of the makers listed here also are represented in the text of this book (see Index).

Names that appear in brackets denote the full names of makers who used initials to brand their work: for example, A[mos] D[enison] Allen, who branded his work "A. D. ALLEN". Many makers who were named James or John branded their work with the initial I., and in these cases, given names also are listed in brackets: for example, I. [James] Always. Spelling variations of last names are provided in parentheses.

Listings that are only initials, rather than full names, are likely to be owners' marks, as opposed to makers' marks, assuming that makers branded their products with their full names so that shippers and purchasers would know who had made them; nonetheless, initials are included on the off-chance that they may be those of a maker whose name is yet to be discovered.

Dates that appear in parentheses indicate years of birth and/or death. Other dates are known working dates, but are not exclusive; that is, a maker may have been working before or after the date or dates shown. A question mark in a listing indicates information that has been deduced from evidence and that, while probably correct, is nonetheless tentative.

Sources that are cited repeatedly are shown below, and are indicated by numbers in parentheses at the ends of the listings. These sources are not intended to be exhaustive, but only as a reference point if you are interested in learning more about certain makers.

The checklist included as Appendix IV of *The Windsor Style in America*—the predecessor of this book—contained several errors of omission and commission which have been corrected in this new list. The following checklist, which includes nearly 100 new names, supersedes the earlier list.

1. Ethel Hall Bjerkoe, *The Cabinetmakers of America.*
2. Charles Dorman, *Delaware Cabinetmakers and Allied Artisans, 1655–1855.*
3. Dean F. Failey, *Long Island Is My Nation.*
4. Dean A. Fales, Jr., *American Painted Furniture 1660–1880.*
5. William Macpherson Hornor, Jr., *Blue Book of Philadelphia Furniture.*
6. Thomas H. Ormsbee, *The Windsor Chair.*
7. *Plain & Elegant, Rich & Common: Documented New Hampshire Furniture, 1750–1850* (New Hampshire Historical Society, Concord).
8. Alfred Coxe Prime, *The Arts and Crafts in Philadelphia, Maryland, and South Carolina, 1721–1785.*
9. Margaret Berwind Schiffer, *Furniture and Its Makers of Chester County, Pennsylvania.*
10. Esther Singleton, *Furniture of Our Forefathers.*
11. *Winterthur Portfolio Thirteen.*
12. "Early Furniture Made in New Jersey, 1690–1870" (catalog of an exhibit at the Newark Museum, October 1958–January 1959).
13. *Antiques* Magazine.
14. *The Maine Antique Digest.*
15. New York Directories.
16. Philadelphia Directories.
17. Personal correspondence.
18. Personal observation.

ACKLEY, I. [JOHN] B[RIETNALL] (1763–1827). Philadelphia, 1791–1802. Worked at 103 N. Front St., 3 Mulberry St., 13 Elfreth's Alley, and 152 N. Front St. "This same Ackley was later a druggist and apothecary, and sold paints," according to Abraham Ritter, *Philadelphia and Her Merchants,* 1860. (16; 17; 18) *See also* TAYLOR and KING

ACKLEY, M. Pennsylvania?, c. 1790. An Ackley chair is in the collection of the Northampton County (Pennsylvania) Historical Society. (17)

ALLEN, A[MOS] D[ENISON] (1744–1855). Lisbon and Norwich, Connecticut (1796–1855). Apprenticed to Ebenezer Tracy; married Tracy's daughter and opened his own shop in 1796. (1; 18) *See also* GREEN, B.

ALLEN, JOB A. White Creek, New York, early nineteenth century. (13:May 1981)

ALLEN, THOMAS. *See* BATES and ALLEN

ALLING, DAVID (1773–1855). Newark, New Jersey, 1800–1850. Also made fancy chairs; the New Jersey Historical Society has a painting titled *David Alling's House and Shop, Newark.* (1; *Sentinel of Freedom* 1808–1809)

ALLVINE (ALLWINE?), JOHN. Baltimore, 1796. (10)

ALLWINE, JOHN. Philadelphia, 1801–1809. Worked at 3 Gray's Alley, 137 S. Front St., 258 N. Second St., and 43 Sassafrass St. (16)

ALLWINE, L[AWRENCE]. Philadelphia, 1786–1799. Worked at 99 S. Front St. and made chairs for Governor John Penn. (5; 16; 18)

ALWAYS, JAMES. New York City, 1786–1815. Worked at 40 James St. (1; 13:May 1981; *New York Weekly Museum,* 28 February 1801)

ALWAYS, I. [JAMES] and HAMTON, I. New York City, 1792 (according to research, in partnership only one year). (13:May 1981; 18)

ALWAYS, JOHN. New York City, 1786–1815. Worked with his brother, James. (1)

ANDREWS, JOEL. Canadaigua, New York, 1804. (17; *Western Repository,* 6 November 1804)

ASH, THOMAS. New York City, 1774. Worked on Broadway. (1; 10; *Rivington's Gazetteer,* 17 February 1774) *See also* TWEED, RICHARD

ASH, TH[OMA]S and WILLIAM. New York City, 1785–1794. Worked at 17 John St.; claimed to make upholstered Windsors in a "mode peculiar to themselves and never before executed in America." (1; 15; *New York Packet,* 3 March 1785; 18)

ASHTON, THOMAS. Philadelphia, c. 1800. (5; 18)

ATWOOD, T. (1785?–1865). Lived in Worcester, Massachusetts, for several years after 1808; opened a chair factory in New Bedford, New Hampshire, in 1819; opened a furniture warehouse in Nashua, New Hampshire, in 1832, where he sold "flag bottomed, Fancy & Common CHAIRS, of all kinds, by the set or hundreds"; sold his property in 1840; moved to Nunda, New York, and in 1860 to Canaseraga, New York. (7; 18)

AUSTIN, D. Mount Vernon, Maine, c. 1810. Painted signature, plus a drawing of a cat. (17)

AUSTIN, RICHARD (1744–1826). Charlestown and Salem, Massachusetts, 1765?–1826. (1)

B

B., R. Philadelphia?, c. 1765–1780. (Brand on a pair of low-back chairs with cylinder-and-ball feet in the collection of Independence National Historical Park, purchased in New York State; may be an owner's mark)

BAILEY, O., JR. New England, c. 1790. (17)

BALCH, ISRAEL, JR. (d. 1809). Mansfield, Connecticut, c. 1790. (17)

BARNARD, JULIUS. Northampton, Massachusetts, and Windsor, Vermont, 1791–1802. (13:May 1980)

BARNET, S[AMPSON]. Wilmington, Delaware, 1795. Several Barnet chairs are in the collection of the Historical Society of Delaware. (2; 17; 18)

A

B

BATES, WILLIAM and ALLEN, THOMAS. New Bedford, Massachusetts, 1822–1824. Worked on Water St. (13:June 1978)

BEACH, ABRAHAM. Newark, New Jersey, c. 1830. (12)

BEAL, J. New England, c. 1810. (17)

BECK, D. (18; seat of a 1780–1800 Massachusetts sack-back)

BECKWITH, HARRIS. Northampton, Massachusetts, and Marlow, New Hampshire, 1803–1820. (13:May 1980)

BEESLEY, WILLIAM G. (d. 1842). Salem, New Jersey, 1828–1842. Bought Windsor parts from local craftsmen and assembled them in his shop with Elijah Ware. (12)

BELDING & COLLINS. Randolph, Ohio, 1829. (17)

BENDER, L[EWIS]. Philadelphia, 1794. (8; 18)

BERTINE, JAMES. New York City, 1790–1797. Worked on Pearl St. and Queen St. (13:May 1981; 15)

BIGGARD, JOHN. Charleston, South Carolina, 1767. Worked on Queen St.; arrived in Charleston from Philadelphia. (1)

BIRDSEY, JOSEPH, JR. Ridgefield or Huntington, Connecticut, 1790–1805. (17)

BISHOP, G. See TOBEY, D., and BISHOP, G.

BISPHAM, J. M. Pennsylvania?, c. 1810. (18)

BLACKFORD, THOMAS. Boston, c. 1795. (14:November 1979)

BLOOM, J. Bloom's Corner (near Milford), New York, c. 1800. (13:May 1981; 18)

BLOOM, MATTHIAS. New York City, 1787–1793. (5; 11:May 1981)

BOUND, WILLIAM. Philadelphia, 1785. Worked on Walnut St. and Chestnut St. (16)

BOWEN, O. M. Pennsylvania?, 1790. (18; brand on a Pennsylvania knuckle-arm sack-back chair)

BOWEN, W[ILLIAM]. Philadelphia, 1786–1810. Worked at 83 N. Front St. (16; 17; brand on a bow-back side chair with bamboo turnings)

BOWEN, W. (WILLIAM?). Bowenton or Roadstown, New Jersey, 1823. (10)

BROOKS. See HUDSON & BROOKS

BROWN, G. Sterling, Massachusetts, c. 1820. (4)

BROWN, HENRY S. Bangor, Maine, c. 1850. A Brown chair is in the Maine State Museum. (15)

BROWN, JOHN. West Chester, Pennsylvania, 1829. Also made fancy chairs. (9; *Village Record,* 25 March 1829)

BROWN, NATHANIEL. Litchfield, Connecticut, 1797. Made "Windsor, fiddleback, dining room, parlor, kitchen, and children's chairs." (1; *Litchfield Monitor,* 1797)

BROWN, NATHANIEL. Savannah, Georgia, c. 1775–1800. (1)

BUCK, P. New England?, c. 1800. (7)

BULLER, WILLIAM. West Chester, Pennsylvania, 1834. Worked on Gay St.; also made fancy chairs, settees, and rocking chairs. (9; *Village Record,* 18 June 1834)

BURCHALL and WICKERSHAM. West Chester, Pennsylvania, 1822. Also made fancy and rush-bottom chairs. (9; *American Republican,* 14 August 1822)

BURDEN, ALEXANDER. Philadelphia, 1822–1831. (16)

BURDEN, J[OSEPH]. Philadelphia, 1793–1827. Worked at 99 S. Third St. and 90 S. Third St.; in partnership with Francis Trumble in 1796. (16; 17; 18)

BURROWS, SMITH. Cincinnati, Ohio, c. 1810. (17)

C

CAIN, T. New England?, c. 1800–1810. (18; Brand on a vigorously turned rod-back side chair)

CALDWELL, J[OHN]. New York City, 1790s. (15; 18; brand on a New York City continuous-arm chair)

CANNON, FERGUS. Worked at 50 S. Front St., Cincinnati, Ohio, 1819. (17)

CAPEN, WILLIAM, JR. New England?, c. 1810. (17)

CARPENTER, WILLIAM. Philadelphia, 1793. Worked at 296 S. Second St. (8)

CARTER, MINOT (1812–1873). New Ipswich, New Hampshire, c. 1826–1841. Related by marriage to Abijah Wetherbee and Josiah Prescott Wilder; worked at Wilder's chair factory. A set of six Carter chairs is in the collection of The Henry Francis du Pont Winterthur Museum. (7; 18)

CARTERET, D[ANIEL]. Philadelphia, 1793–1820. Worked at 24 Shippen St., 391 S. Front St., and 393 S. Front St. (16; 18)

CASE, A. G. (1769–1828). Norwich, Connecticut, 1790?–1828. (17)

CATE, H. Probably Boston; possibly Rhode Island, c. 1785. (18)

CAULTON, RICHARD. Williamsburg, Virginia, 1745. (Marion Iverson Day, *The American Chair, 1630–1890*)

CHALLEN, WILLIAM. Lexington, Kentucky, 1800; advertised that he had worked in London and New York. (*Kentucky Gazette,* 13 June 1800)

CHAMBERS, DAVID. Philadelphia, 1748. Worked on Walnut St. and Plumb St. (*Pennsylvania Gazette,* 18 August 1748)

CHAMPLIN, H. P. Rhode Island?, c. 1780–1800. (17)

CHAPIN, ELIPHALET. *See* WILLIAMS, EBENEZER

CHAPMAN I. [JOHN]. Philadelphia, 1793–1809. Worked at various addresses on Eighth St. and at 2 Cherry St.; supplied 12 chairs to the Arch Street Meeting House. (16; 17)

CHASE, C. Massachusetts?, c. 1775. (18)

CHESLEY, WILLIAM. Durham, New Hampshire, c. 1800. (7)

CHESNUT. *See* CHESTNUT

CHESTNEY, JAMES. Albany, New York, 1798–1805. Worked at 72 Market St.; also made rush-bottom chairs. (4)

CHESTNUT (CHESNUT), J[ARED]. Wilmington, Delaware, 1804–1814. Was in partnership with James Ross on Hemphill's Wharf in 1804; also worked at 20 Market St. (2)

CHILDRES. *See* POINTER and CHILDRES

CLARK, I. (JOSIAH?). Hartford, Connecticut, c. 1800. (17)

CLARK, OLIVER (b. 1774). Litchfield, Connecticut, 1797. Worked with Ebenezer Plumb, Jr. (1)

CLARK & CROWELL. Cincinnati, Ohio, 1822. Worked on Fourth St. (17)

COFFIN, JOB B. Fishkill, New York, c. 1780. (13:May 1981; 17)

COLE, GEORGE. Baltimore, 1796. (1)

COLE, JACOB. Baltimore, 1796. (10)

COLLINS. *See* BELDING & COLLINS

COMMERFORD, JOHN. Brooklyn, New York, 1829–1832. Worked at 18 Hicks St.; also made fancy chairs. (3)

CONCHITA. Caribbean?, c. 1825. (17; maker's or owner's brand on a simplified rod-back side chair)

CONOVER, MICHAEL F. Philadelphia, 1840. (*Public Ledger,* 14 January 1840)

COUTANT, DAVID. *See* COUTONG

COUTONG (COUTANT), D[AVID]. New York City and New Rochelle, New York, c. 1780–1800. (13:May 1981; 15; brand on the front of the seat pommel of a continuous-arm chair, 1790–1810)

COVERT, ISAAC. Philadelphia, 1772–1786. Apprenticed to Joseph Henzey in 1772. (5)

COWPERTHWAITE, JOHN K. New York City, 1815. Also made fancy chairs. (New York Historical Society)

COX, W[ILLIAM] (d. 1811). Newcastle, Delaware, and Philadelphia, 1767–c. 1804. Worked on Second St.; also made rush-bottom chairs; supplied Stephen Girard with more than 40 dozen Windsors for shipment; used punch marks as shown here as well as his name to brand his chairs. (5; 16; 17)
A. Brand of William Cox.
B. Punch marks of William Cox.

A

B

CROWELL. *See* CLARK & CROWELL

CUBBIN. *See* WEAR and CUBBIN

CURTIS and HUBBARD [J. C.?]. Boston, 1828. Also made fancy chairs. (1)

CUSTER, J[ESSE]. Vincent and Coventry Townships, Chester County, Pennsylvania, 1796–1798. (9)

D

DANNLEY, G. D. Pine Grove, Pennsylvania, c. 1825. (18)

DAVID, S. *See* WEST and DAVID

DAVIS, W. *See* RAMSEY and DAVIS

DAVIS, WILLIAM. Philadelphia, 1791. Worked at 28 Branch St. (8)

DEGANT, JOSEPH. Halifax, Nova Scotia, c. 1790

DEGROAT, JOHN. New Brunswick, New Jersey, 1791. (12; *Brunswick Gazette,* 9 August 1791)

DE WITT, JOHN. New York City, 1794–1799. Worked at 38 Whitehall St., 225 William St., 47 Water St., and 442 Pearl St.; made Windsors for the Senate and Assembly rooms, Federal Hall, New York City. (4; 15)

DILLER, R. Pennsylvania?, c. 1800. (18)

DIX, E. New Hampshire? or Maine?, c. 1790. (18; brand on a carved-ear fan-back side chair)

DOAK, WILLIAM. Boston, 1789. Worked on Back St.; also a cabinet-maker. (1)

DODGE. New England?, c. 1810. (14: October 1976; brand on a pair of braced bow-back side chairs)

DOMINY, NATHANIEL, V (1770–1852). East Hampton, New York, c. 1780–1840. Made a wide variety of furniture; the Dominy shop and tools are in the collection of The Henry Francis du Pont Winterthur Museum. (3)

DOW, I. (18; brand on a Rhode Island-style bow-back side chair, 1800–1820)

DUNBAR, GEORGE. Canton, Ohio, 1817. Advertised that he made "common Windsor chairs." (17)

DUNHAM, CAMPBELL. New Brunswick, New Jersey, 1793–1805. Worked on Albany St.; also made fancy and rush-bottom chairs. (12)

DUPRAY, F. New England?, c. 1820. (17)

E

EDLING, JOHN. Philadelphia, 1797. Worked on S. Second St. (16)

EDWARDS, BENJAMIN A. (1773–1822). Northampton, Massachusetts, 1790–1822. (13:May 1980)

EUSTACE. Connecticut?, c. 1800. (Brand on a comb-back chair)

EVANS, E[PHRAIM]. Philadelphia, 1785, and Alexandria, Virginia, 1786. In Philadelphia, worked on Front St. (1; 16; 17)

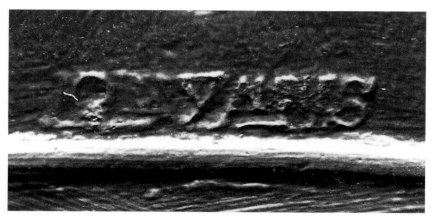

F

F., C., JR. Pennsylvania?, c. 1790. Possibly an owner's mark. (17)

FETTER, I. [JACOB] (1756–1833) and FREDERICK. Lancaster, Pennsylvania, until 1833. (13:May 1979)

FINLAY, JOHN and HUGH. Baltimore, 1803–1833. Made a wide variety of furniture. (4)

FITTS. *See* SPOONER & FITTS

FLINT. *See* WELLS and FLINT

FOLSOM, JOSIAH (1763–1837). Portsmouth, New Hampshire, 1788–1812. Advertised in the *New Hampshire Gazette* (Portsmouth) 19 September 1797 that he "made & kept for sale [Windsor chairs] as cheap as can be purchased at BOSTON or elsewhere"; may have apprenticed in Boston. (7)

FOSTER, J[ESSE]. Boston, 1796. Also a cabinetmaker. (1)

FOX, WILLIAM. Philadelphia, 1796. Worked at 50 N. Front St. (16)

FRANCIS, WILLIAM. Philadelphia, 1791–1800. Worked at 69 Green St., N. Third St., and Race St. (16)

FRAZER. (18; brand on a Pennsylvania "duckbill" child's side chair with bamboo turnings, 1810–1820)

FREEMAN, BENJAMIN, and HOUCK, ANDREW. Philadelphia, 1784. Worked on Front St.; also made rush-bottom chairs. (*Pennsylvania Journal*, 4 September 1784)

FRENCH, JOHN, II. New London, Connecticut, 1807. (1; *Connecticut Gazette*, 18 February 1807)

FROST. *See* SEAVER and FROST

FRY, GEORGE. Philadelphia, 1800?–1820. (4; 16)

G

GALER, ADAM. New York City, 1774. Moved to New York City from Philadelphia. (*Rivington's Gazetteer*, 2 September 1774)

GALLUP, WILLIAM. Norwalk, Ohio, 1830. (17)

GAMMON, G. Halifax, Nova Scotia, c. 1800. (14:June 1981)

GAUTIER, ANDREW. New York City, 1746–1766. Worked on Princess St. (15; *New York Journal*, 13 February 1766)

GAW, GILBERT. Philadelphia, 1798–1824. Worked at 90 N. Front St. and 84 N. Front St. (5; 16; 17) *See also* GAW, GILBERT & ROBERT
A. Brand on a bow-back side chair.
B. Gaw used this label while he was working at 90 N. Front St. in Philadelphia.

A

B

GAW, G[ILBERT] & R[OBERT]. Philadelphia, 1793–1798. Worked at 34 Elfreth's Alley. (5; 16; 17)

GAW, R[OBERT]. Philadelphia, 1798–1839. Worked at various addresses on Front St. (5; 16; 17) *See also* GAW, GILBERT and ROBERT

GEYER, JOHN; KERR [?]; and ROSS, WILLIAM H. Cincinnati, Ohio, 1831–1841. Operated the Western Chair Manufactory [sic] at 19 W. Third St. (17)

GIDEON, GEORGE. Philadelphia, 1799–1820. Worked on Slaughter's Court, 33 Vine St., and 202 N. Eighth St. (16)

GILBERT, JABEZ. Windham, Connecticut, 1769. (1)

GILLINGHAM, W. (WILLIAM?) (1783–1850). Morrisville, Pennsylvania, 1800?–1850? (17; 18)

GILPIN, T[HOMAS] (1700–1766). Birmingham and Thornbury Townships, Chester County, Pennsylvania, and Philadelphia, 1735?–1766. Maker of some of the earliest-known branded Windsors. (5; 9; 17)

GOLDSBURY & MUSSER. Canton, Ohio, 1818. (17)

GLADDING, J[ONATHAN]. Newport, R.I., c. 1770. Brand on a braced, bow-back, tenon-arm Rhode Island-style Windsor chair with pipestem spindles. (1; 13: February 1987 advertisement)

GOODRICH, ANSEL. Northampton, Massachusetts, 1795–1803. The Northampton (Massachusetts) Historical Society has two Goodrich chairs in its collection. (13:May 1980)

GORDON, JOHN. Baltimore, 1833. Worked at 41 Water St. (1)

GRAGG, SAMUEL. Boston, 1808–1833. Also made a unique form of bentwood fancy chair. (3)

GRANT & JEMISON. Lexington, Kentucky, 1807. Worked on Main St.; apparently Jemison was a chairmaker and Grant a painter. (*Kentucky Gazette,* 15 December 1807)

GRAY, I. Massachusetts; probably Boston. (Brand on a bow-back, cross-stretcher side chair, probably Boston, 1790–1815; 18)

GREEN, B. South Windham, Connecticut, c. 1810–1820. An apprentice of A. D. Allen (17)

GREEN, JACOB. Philadelphia, 1823 (16)

H

HAGGET, AMOS. Charlestown, Massachusetts, c. 1815. A Hagget chair is in the collection of The Henry Francis du Pont Winterthur Museum.

HAHN, A. (18; brand on a fan-back side chair, possibly Philadelphia or Bucks County, Pennsylvania, 1760–1780)

HALL, RICHARD. Halifax, North Carolina, 1770 (6)

HALL, WILLIAM. Sag Harbor, New York, 1802–1804. Also a cabinet-maker. (3)

HALLET, JAMES, JR. New York City, 1801. Worked at 8 John St. (*New York Gazette and General Advertiser,* 22 October 1801)

HAMILTON, BENJAMIN. Solebury, Pennsylvania, 1809. Also made "patent churns." (*Pennsylvania Correspondent,* 20 April 1809)

HAMTON, I. *See* ALWAYS and HAMTON

HAND, RICHARD. Bridgeton, New Jersey, 1826. Also made fancy chairs. (11)

HANNAH, CALEB. Baltimore and Fell's Point, Maryland, 1796. (1)

HARBISON, WILLIAM. Wilmington, Delaware, 1814. Worked at 46 King St. (*Porter's Register*)

HARDWICK, JAMES. Lexington, Kentucky, 1794. (1)

HARRIS, WILLIAM, JR. New London, Connecticut, 1788. (1; 18; *New London Gazette,* 14 November 1788)

HARVEY, D. Passumsic?, Vermont?, c. 1810. (17; brand on the bottom of a Windsor cradle)

HASBROUCK, J. M. Kingston, New York, 1800. (13: May 1981; 15)

HAYS, THOMAS. New York City, 1800. (*Daily Advertiser,* 3 November 1800)

HAYWARD, THOMAS COTTON. Charlestown, Massachusetts, 1770–1800. (Robert Bishop, *The American Chair 1640–1770*)

HEINY, C[HRISTIAN]. Philadelphia, 1791. Worked at 496 N. Second St. (16; brand on a bow-back, Philadelphia-style side chair with bamboo turnings) (Heiny's name was misspelled in the earlier checklist contained in *The Windsor Style in America* due to an apparent typographical error in the original research material.)

HENZEY, I. [JOSEPH] (b. 1743). Philadelphia, 1760?–1806? Worked at 106 S. Eighth St. and 76 Almond St.; made chairs for the Library Company, the State Assembly, and the First Bank of America. Occasionally, the initials I. H. are branded on the later bamboo-turned tenon-arm Henzey chairs. (5; 16; 17)

A   B

HERRCK (HERRICK?), S. N. Rhode Island?, c. 1780. (18)

HEWS, ALPHEUS. New Jersey and New Haven, Connecticut, 1787. In New Haven, worked on Chapel St. (1; 6)

HIGBEE and WALL. Philadelphia, 1800. Worked next to 10 N. Front St. (16)

HOLMES, ISAAC. Lexington and Frankfort, Kentucky, 1806–1808. (1)

HOOVER, JACOB. Kendall (Massillon), Ohio, 1817. Operated a Windsor chair factory. (17)

HOPPER, NICHOLAS. Philadelphia, 1795–1796. Worked at 38 High St. (16)

HORN (HORNE), JACOB. Philadelphia, 1797–1800. Worked on Cherry St. and Fifth St. (16)

HORN, SAMUEL. Canton, Ohio, 1835. (17)

HORTON, S. (SAMUEL?). Boston?, c. 1807. (1; 17)

HOUCK, ANDREW. *See* FREEMAN and HOUCK

HOUGH, M. Cleveland, 1848. (17)

HOXIE. Rhode Island?, c. 1790. (17; brand on a brace-back armchair)

HUBBARD, J. C., and WHITE, WILLIAM. Boston, c. 1800. (18) *See also* CURTIS and HUBBARD

HUDSON & BROOKS. Portland, Maine, c. 1815–1823. (*Newtown Bee,* August 26, 1983)

HUEY, JAMES (b. 1805). Zanesville, Ohio, c. 1830–1840. (*Ohio Republican,* 21 May 1829; Columbus Museum of Art, *Made in Ohio: Furniture 1788–1888*)

HUMMESTON, J[AY]. Delaware; Charleston, South Carolina, 1798–1802; and Halifax, Nova Scotia, 1804. (14; 17)

HUMMESTON, JAY, and STAFFORD, THEODORE. Charleston, South Carolina, 1798. (1; *Charlestown City Gazette and Advertiser,* 29 November 1798)

HUMPHREYVILLE, J. D. Morristown, New Jersey, 1828. Also made fancy chairs. (12)

HUNT, J[OSEPH] R[UGGLES] (1781–1871). Eaton (Madison), New Hampshire, c. 1811–1860. Born in Boston, Hunt may have apprenticed there. (7)

HURDLE, LEVI. Alexandria, Virginia, 1835. Worked on King St. in partnership with his brother, Thomas; also made fancy chairs. (1, *Alexandria Gazette,* 1 January 1835)

HUTCHINS, ZADOCK. Pomfret, Connecticut, c. 1820. A Hutchins chair is in the collection of The Henry Francis du Pont Winterthur Museum (18)

I

ILSLEY, G. L./EXETER. Exeter, New Hampshire, c. 1800. (18; brand on a rod-back side chair)

INMAN. American, nineteenth century. (17)

INTLE. *See* LECOCK and INTLE

J

JACQUES (JAQUES), RICHARD. New Brunswick, New Jersey, c. 1775. Also made spinning wheels. (12)

JEFFERIS, JAMES and EMMOR. West Chester, Pennsylvania, 1830. Worked on Church St. (*Village Record,* 20 January 1830)

JEFFERIS, NATHAN (1773–1823). East Bradford Township, Chester County, Pennsylvania, c. 1800. (Chester County Historical Society)

JEMISON. *See* GRANT & JEMISON

JOHNSON and TATEM. Bridgeton, New Jersey, 1856. (11)

JUDD, DAVID. Northampton, Massachusetts, 1799–1827. Made a wide variety of furniture. (13:May 1980)

K

KELSO, JOHN. New York City, 1774. Served his apprenticeship in Philadelphia. (1; 6)

KERR. *See* GEYER, KERR, and ROSS

KILBURN (KILBOURNE), S. New London, Ohio, c. 1840. (17; S-KILBOURNE brand appears on a set of thumb-back side chairs)

KING, JESSE. Philadelphia, c. 1770. (5)

KING, PELEG C. Southold, New York, 1804. Also made rush-bottom chairs. (3)

KITCHEL (KITCHELL), ISAAC. New York City, 1789–1812. (3)

KITLER, JOHN L. (16)

L

LAMBERT, JOHN. Philadelphia, c. 1760–1793. His shop had "3 Machines for letting in feet with Propriety & Dispatch." (5)

LAWRENCE, DANIEL. Providence, Rhode Island, 1787. Worked on Westminster St. (1)

LEAGUE, REUBEN. Baltimore, 1796. (10)

LECOCK and INTLE. New York City, 1786. (10)

LEDYARD. Massachusetts?, c. 1790–1810. (18; brand on a sack-back chair)

LEE, JOHN. Newark, New Jersey, 1827–1855? Also made fancy chairs. (12)

LEIGH, JOHN. Trenton, New Jersey, c. 1790. Worked at 107 Factory St.; also a cabinetmaker. (18)

LETCHWORTH, I. [JOHN] (b. 1759). Philadelphia, 1785–1824. Worked on Third St. and at 76 and 78 S. Fourth St.; one of the most prolific of Philadelphia makers; made chairs for the New City Hall. (5; 11)

LEWIS, C. Pennsylvania?, c. 1800. (18; brand on a Pennsylvania-style rod-back chair)

LLOYD, RICHARD. Cincinnati, Ohio, 1830s. Worked on Third St. (17)

LOCKE, HENRY. New York?, c. 1790. (18)

LOVE, B[ENJAMIN]. Philadelphia, 1783–1802. (17)

LOVE, W[ILLIAM]. Philadelphia, 1793–1806. Worked at 150 N. Front St. and 216 N. Second St.; also made spinning wheels; a Love chair is in the collection of Independence National Historical Park. (16)

LOVE and WHITELOCK. Philadelphia, c. 1790. (18)

LOW, HENRY V. New Brunswick, New Jersey, 1804. Worked on Albany St.; also made fancy and rush-bottom chairs. (12)

LUTHER, NATHAN. Salem, Massachusetts, and Providence, Rhode Island, 1810–1837. (1; 14:May 1978)

M

MACBRIDE, W[ALTER]. New York City, 1792–1799. (13: May 1981; brand on a continuous-arm brace-back armchair)

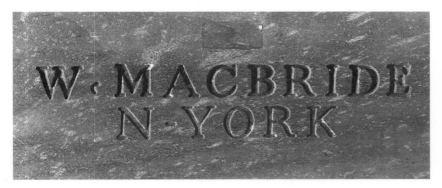

MACY, JOSIAH. Hudson, New York, c. 1810. (13:May 1981; 17)

MCADAN, THOMAS F. Philadelphia, 1820. (16)

MCCORMICK, S. Connecticut?, c. 1790–1810. (18; brand on a fan-back side chair)

MCELROY, W[ILLIAM]. Camden, New Jersey, 1790–1800. (17; 18)

M'KIM, ANDREW and ROBERT. Richmond, Virginia, 1802–1819. (1; Museum of Early Southern Decorative Arts)

M'PHERSON, ALEXANDER. Philadelphia, 1793. Worked at 16 George St. (16)

MANNING, CALEB (d. 1810). Salem, Massachusetts, 1803–1810. Worked on Daniel, Federal, Fish, and Derby Sts. (1)

MANSFIELD. Connecticut?, c. 1780. (17)

MARCH, JONES. Lexington, Kentucky, 1833. Also made fancy chairs. (1; *Lexington Observer and Kentucky Reporter,* 21 August 1833)

MARSH, CHARLES. New York City, c. 1800. Worked at 75 John St. (1; 13:May 1930)

MARSH, RICHARD. New York City, 1806. Worked on Greenwich St.; also made fancy chairs. (10)

MARTIN, JACOB. Philadelphia, 1785–1801. Worked on Third St. and at 87 N. Front St.; also a joiner and cabinetmaker. (5; 16)

MASON, JOHN. Philadelphia, 1811. Worked at 49 Pine St. (5; 16)

MASON, T[HOMAS]. Philadelphia, 1793–1817. Worked at 169 N. Third St., various addresses on Vine St., and at 20 Callowhill St. (16; 18)

MASON, WILLIAM. Philadelphia, 1794. Worked at 60 Vine St. (16)

MATTOCKS, JOHN. Litchfield, Connecticut, 1797. Advertised that he would take "bass wood plank" for chair seats in exchange for his work. (1)

METCALF, LUTHER (1765–1838). Medway, Massachusetts, 1770–1838. Apprenticed to Elisha Richardson, 1770–1778. (1) ·

MILLARD, THOMAS. Philadelphia, 1791–1819. A maker of Windsor chairs and spinning wheels; worked at 128 and 129 S. Water St. in 1791, and at 398 N. Front St. from 1793 to 1800. (16)

MILLER, JOHN. Baltimore, 1796. (10)

MILLS, JOHN. Chillicothe, Ohio, 1842. Also made fancy chairs. (17)

MITCHELL, WILLIAM. Philadelphia, 1799–1817. Worked at various addresses on Lombard St. and at 10 Union St. (16)

MOON, DAVID. *See* MOON, SAMUEL, and MOON, WILLIAM D.

MOON, SAMUEL. Philadelphia, 1800–1802. Worked at 2 Carter's Alley, and, with David Moon, at 66 S. Fourth St. (16)

MOON, WILLIAM D. Philadelphia and Crewcorne (Morrisville, Bucks County), Pennsylvania, 1799–1829. In Philadelphia, worked at 19 Dock St., 299 N. Second St., 32 N. Fourth St., and, with David Moon, at 18 Carter's Alley. (16; 17)

MOON, WILLIAM D., and PRALL, EDWARD. Philadelphia, 1805. Worked at 63 S. Front St. (16; 17)

MOROW, PETER. Philadelphia, 1820. (16)

MORRIS. *See* WORREL and MORRIS

MORSE, R. New England?, c. 1810. (14:November 1984)

MOTZER, A. Connecticut?, c. 1790. (18)

MUCKE, S. Ontario, Canada, and/or northern New England, 1760?–1800? (14)

MURPHY, MICHAEL. Philadelphia, 1793–1800. (16)

MUSSER. See GOLDSBURY & MUSSER

N

NELSON, O. Connecticut?, c. 1790. (18; brand on a sack-back chair)

NEWCOMB. *See* WHITAKER and NEWCOMB

NEWMAN, BENJAMIN. Gloucester, Massachusetts, 1815–1825. (4)

NICHOLS, JOSEPH. Savannah, Georgia, 1800. (1)

NICHOLS, SAMUEL. Wilmington, Delaware, 1800. Worked in partnership with George Young at Second and King Sts. (2) *See also* YOUNG, GEORGE.

NORTON, JACOB. Hartford, Connecticut, 1790. (1; *American Mercury,* 8 November 1790)

O

ODELL, REUBEN. New York City, 1815–1836. Worked on Barkley, Duane, Chambers, Rivington, and Bowery Sts. (15; 17)

OGILBY, J. Pennsylvania?, c. 1770–1790. (18; brand on a Philadelphia-style sack-back chair)

OLDHAM, JOHN. Baltimore, 1796. (10)

ORMSBY, ORRIN (b. 1766). Windham, Connecticut, c. 1785. (1)

OSSBACK (OSBECK), JOHN. Philadelphia, 1817–1820. Worked on Adelphia Ave., at 97 N. Front St., and 2 M'Culloch's Court. (16)

P

PACKARD, S. H. Rochester, New York, 1819. (17)

PAINE, S. [STEPHEN?] C. 1760, possibly Charlestown and Medford, Massachusetts, 1743–1752. (18; brand on a comb-back chair)

PAINE, S. [STEPHEN?] O. Philadelphia, c. 1760, or possibly Charlestown and Medford, Massachusetts, 1743–1752. (1; 18; brand on a Philadelphia-style low-back armchair)

PARSONS, JUSTIN. Westhampton, Massachusetts, 1796–1807. (13:May 1980)

PARSONS, THEODOSIUS. Windham, Connecticut, 1792. Also a cabinetmaker. (1; *Connecticut Gazette,* 18 October 1792)

PEARSON, GEORGE (b. 1789). West Chester, Pennsylvania, 1810?–1817. (9)

PEASE, J. M. Connecticut?, c. 1789. (Patricia Kane, *300 Years of American Seating Furniture*)

PENTLAND I. [JAMES]. Philadelphia, 1791–1806. Worked at various addresses from 221 to 227 N. Front St. (16)

PHIPPEN, SAMUEL (d. 1798). Salem, Massachusetts, c. 1785. (10)

PINKERTON, JOHN. Philadelphia, 1779. Made two settees for the Courtroom at Independence Hall. (5)

PLUMB, EBENEZER, JR. *See* CLARK, OLIVER

POINTER and CHILDRES. Richmond, Virginia, c. 1782. (1)

POMEROY, OLIVER. Northampton, Massachusetts, and Buffalo, New York, 1795–1818. (13:May 1980)

PRALL, EDWARD. Philadelphia, 1805–1820. Worked at 56 and 64 N. Sixth St. and at 72 N. Fifth St. (16) *See also* MOON, WILLIAM D., and PRALL, EDWARD

PRALL, HENRY. Philadelphia, 1798–1802. Worked at 8, 15, and 17 Dock St. (16)

PRATT, JOEL, JR. Sterling, Massachusetts, c. 1835. A Pratt chair is in the collection of the Henry Ford Museum. (1)

PRESCOTT, LEVI (1777–1823). Boylston, Massachusetts, 1799. A Prescott chair is in the collection of Old Sturbridge Village. (13:October 1979)

PRUYN, JOHN V. L. New York?, c. 1800. (18; maker's or owner's brand on a child's bow-back side chair with bamboo turnings)

PUGH, S. Pennsylvania, c. 1810. (14:September 1979; 18)

R

R., J. N. Philadelphia?, c. 1765–1780. (18; brand on a Philadelphia-style low-back armchair with blunt-arrow feet)

RAIN, THOMAS. Philadelphia, 1799–1814. Worked at various addresses on Front St. and at 135 N. Water St. and 15 Coombs Alley. (16)

RAMSEY, T., and DAVIS, W./PITTSBURGH, c. 1790. (17; brand on a pair of bow-back side chairs)

RAYBOLD, THOMAS. Philadelphia, 1823. (16)

REDMOND, ANDREW (d. 1791). Charleston, South Carolina, 1784–1791. Worked at 27 Meeting St. (1; *South Carolina Gazette,* 13 January 1784)

REED, E. New England?, c. 1825. (14:September 1984)

RICHARDSON, ELISHA. Franklin, Massachusetts, 1743–1798. (1)

RICHMONDE. Philadelphia, 1763. (5)

RILEY [?], & ROBINSON, JOHN. Wilmington, Delaware, 1811. (2)

ROBERTS, S. New Mills, New Jersey, c. 1810. (12)

ROBINSON (ROBISON), JOHN. Wilmington, Delaware, 1811. Worked on Front St., two doors from Market St. (2) *See also* RILEY & ROBINSON

ROGERS, M. New York or Connecticut, c. 1780–1800. (18; brand on a sack-back Windsor)

ROSE, E. P. New England?, c. 1810. (13:November 1979)

ROSS, JAMES. *See* CHESTNUT, JARED

ROSS, WILLIAM H. *See* GEYER, KERR, and ROSS

RUSSEL, WILLIAM, JR. New Bedford, Massachusetts, c. 1800. Worked on Union St. (6; *American Collector,* 6 September 1934)

S

SAGE, LEWIS. Middletown, Connecticut, and Northampton, Massachusetts, 1790?–1822. (13:May 1980)

SAMLER, I. New York, c. 1780. (17)

SANBORN [REUBEN], BOSTON. Boston, 1799. (1; 14: October 1979; brand on a pair of rod-back side chairs with bamboo turnings)
A. Brand of Reuben Sanborn.
B. Chalk signature of Reuben Sanborn.

SCHUMM, J. [JACOB?]. Pennsylvania?, c. 1810. (14:February 1981; 17; brand on a set of rod-back chairs with bamboo turnings)

SCOTT, EDWARD. Boston, 1801. (1)

SEAVER, WILLIAM. Boston, 1789–1896. (1; 10; at left of brand is a large "O"[?])
A. Brand of William Seaver.
B. Label and brand of William Seaver on seat bottom.

SEAVER, WILLIAM, and FROST, JAMES. Boston, 1798. (1; 10; 13:January 1957)

SHARPLESS, BENJAMIN (1748–1833). Bridgeton, New Jersey, and Chester County, Pennsylvania, c. 1810. (12; Schiffer, *Miniature Furniture*)

SHAW, AARON. Plumstead (Plumsteadville), Pennsylvania, 1806. Also made spinning wheels. (*Pennsylvania Correspondent*, 31 March 1806)

SHEPPARD, C. Philadelphia?, c. 1810. (18; brand on a Philadelphia-style rod-back armchair)

SHERALD, JOSIAH. Philadelphia, 1765. Worked on Second St.; also made rush-bottom chairs. (*Pennsylvania Gazette*, 5 September 1765)

SHIPMAN, WILLIAM. Middletown, Connecticut, 1785. (1)

SHOUSE, I. Pennsylvania?, c. 1820. (17)

SHREADER, I. Pennsylvania?, c. 1790. (18)

SHUREMAN, WILLIAM. New York City, 1817. Worked at 17 Bowery St.; also made fancy chairs. (10)

SIMMS, ISAAC. P. Massachusetts, c. 1780. (1)

SKELLORN, GEORGE W., FANCY WINDSOR CHAIRMAKER. New York City, 1800–1827. Worked at 356 Pearl St. (18; label on a bamboo rod-back armchair, one of a set of two armchairs and four side chairs)

SMALL, ISAAC. Newport, Rhode Island, 1803. Worked on Marlborough St. (1)

SMITH, CARMAN. Huntington, New York, 1826. Also made fancy chairs. (3)

SMITH, THOMAS. West Chester, Pennsylvania, 1842. Worked on Church St. (9)

SMITH, WILLIAM V. Brooklyn, New York, 1826. Also made fancy chairs. (3)

SNOWDEN, JEDEDIAH. Philadelphia, 1748. Was also a cabinetmaker. (5)

SNYDER, ADAM. Philadelphia, 1798–1820. Worked on Brown, Green, and Third Sts.; also made fancy chairs. (16)

SNYDER, WILLIAM. Philadelphia, 1793–1801. Worked on Brown St. and Third St. (16)

SPOONER & FITTS. Athol, Massachusetts, c. 1800. (18; brand on a rod-back side chair)

SPRINER. Probably Pennsylvania, c. 1810–20. (18; brand on a bow-back side chair with bamboo turnings)

SPROSON (SPROSEN, SPROWSON), I. [JOHN]. Philadelphia, 1783–1788, and New York City, 1789–1798. (5; 8; 15; 16; brand on a braced bow-back side chair)

STACKHOUSE, DAVID. Philadelphia, 1772. Was apprenticed to Joseph Henzey in 1772. (5)

STACKHOUSE, STACY. Hartford, Connecticut, 1786–1792. Moved to Hartford from New York City. (1; *Connecticut Courant,* 30 January 1786) *See also* WADSWORTH, JOHN

STAFFORD, THEODORE. Charleston, South Carolina, 1801. Worked at 98 Tradd St. (1) *See also* HUMMESTON and STAFFORD

STALCUP, ISRAEL. Wilmington, Delaware, 1798. (*Delaware Gazette,* 24 March 1798)

STANYAN, J. (18; brand on a Pennsylvania Windsor stool, 1790–1820)

STEEL, A[NTHONY]. Philadelphia, 1791–1817. Worked at various addresses on S. Wharves, Spruce St., Little Dock St., and S. Second St. (16)

STEWART, DANIEL. Farmington, Maine, 1812–1827. (17)

STEWART, DAVID. Philadelphia, 1797. Worked on Eighth St. (16)

STIBBS, SAMUEL. Cincinnati, Ohio, 1819. Worked at 107 Main St. (17)

STONE, EBENEZER (b. 1793). Boston, 1787. (1)

STONER, MICHAEL. Lancaster or Berks County, Pennsylvania, c. 1770. (18)

STOUT,[S] C. Pennsylvania?, c. 1790. Stout chairs have been found in the Reading, Pennsylvania, area. (18; brand on a bow-back side chair with bamboo turnings)

STOW, J[OHN] PHIL[A] *fecit.* Philadelphia, c. 1780. (18; brand on a fan-back side chair)

SWAN, OLIVER. Otsego County (Cooperstown area), New York.

SWANN, E. New England?, c. 1790. (18)

SWIFT, R[EUBEN] W[ILLIAM] (or REUBEN and WILLIAM). New Bedford, Massachusetts, 1800–1825. (13:May 1978)

T

TATEM. *See* JOHNSON and TATEM

TAYLOR, N. New England?, c. 1810. (17)

TAYLOR, ROBERT. Philadelphia, 1799?–1817. (16; 17)

TAYLOR and KING, Philadelphia, c. 1800. Successors to John B. Ackley. (5)

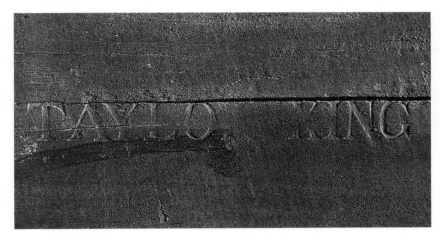

TENNY, S. Rhode Island?, c. 1790. (17)

TERRY, L. E. Boston?, c. 1780. (Marsh, *The Easy Expert in American Antiques*)

THAYER, A. New Jersey?, c. 1800. (18; brand on a low-back writing-arm chair)

THORNTON, J. Pennsylvania?, c. 1765. (18)

TIMPSON (TIMPSON), THOMAS. New York City, 1801. (13:May 1981)

TOBEY, D. [DANIEL?], and BISHOP, G. [GEORGE?]. Maine, c. 1810. (17)

TOMKINS, SQUIER. Morristown, New Jersey, 1808–1812. Worked on Bridge St.; also made fancy chairs. (12; *Genius of Liberty,* 24 November 1808)

TOOKER, BENJAMIN. Elizabethtown, New Jersey, 1820–1830. Worked with A. Tooker, Jr.; also made fancy chairs. (12; *New Jersey Journal,* 2 February 1830)

TOV, P. S. Philadelphia?, 1800–1820. (18; brand on the back of the crest medallion of a Philadelphia rod-back armchair)

TRACY, E[LIJAH] (1766–1807). Lisbon, Connecticut, 1790s. Was a tenant on land owned by his father, Ebenezer Tracy. (17)

A

B

TRACY, E[BENEZER] B. (1744–1803) Lisbon, Connecticut, 1764?–1803. One of the most prolific makers of Windsors, Tracy seems to have specialized in writing-arm chairs. (13:December 1936; 18)

TRACY, S. Connecticut, c. 1790. (18)

TROVILLO, P. New England?, c. 1800. (18)

TRUMBLE, F[RANCIS] (1716?–1798). Philadelphia, 1740?–1798. Worked at various addresses on Front St. and Second St.; made a wide variety of furniture and other items; made 78 Windsors for the State House and 12 chairs for the House of Representatives. The brand on his earlier furniture (figure A) differs from one he used later (figure B). (5; 18; *Winterthur Portfolio One*)
A. Brand on a fan-back side chair with vase-and-ring turnings, c. 1765.
B. Brand on a bow-back side chair with bamboo turnings, c. 1780.

A

B

TUCKE (TUCK), S[AMUEL] J. Boston, 1790–1796. Worked on Battery March St.; a Tucke chair is in the collection of Colonial Williamsburg. (1; 17; *Massachusetts Sentinel,* March 1790)

TUFTS, U[RIAH]. Rhode Island, c. 1785. (17; 18)

TUTTLE, J[AMES] C[HAPMAN] (1772?–1849). Salem, Massachusetts, 1796. Worked on Federal St.; was also a cabinetmaker. (1; *Salem Gazette,* 19 August 1796)

TWEED, RICHARD (b. 1790). New York City, c. 1815. Worked at 24 Cherry St.; served his apprenticeship with Thomas Ash. (1; 6)

V

VANHORN, NATHANIEL. Philadelphia, 1820–1823. (16)

VOSBURGH, HERMAN. New York City, 1785?–1800. (16; *New York Weekly Museum,* 29 March 1800)

W

W., P. N. Rhode Island?, c. 1790. (18; the owner's or maker's brand on a Rhode Island-style continuous-arm chair)

WADSWORTH, JOHN. Hartford, Connecticut, 1793–1796. Took over the shop of Stacy Stackhouse; made furniture for the Old State House. (1; *American Mercury,* 10 June 1793)

WALL. *See* HIGBEE and WALL

WALL, JOHN (JONATHAN). Philadelphia, 1805–1820. Worked at various addresses on N. Front St.; also made fancy chairs. (16)

WARD, JOSEPH. New Brunswick, New Jersey, 1796–1798. Worked on Church St. and Albany St. (12; *The Guardian,* 28 June 1796)

WARE, ELIJAH. *See* BEESLEY, WILLIAM G.

WARNER, EVERADUS. Brooklyn, New York, 1801. (3; *Long Island Courier,* 18 November 1801)

WATERHOUSE, TIMOTHY. Newport, Rhode Island, c. 1764. A set of 12 low-back chairs in the collection of the Redwood Library and Atheneum is attributed to Waterhouse. (Redwood Library and Atheneum)

WEAR and CUBBIN. Philadelphia, 1785. Worked on Water St. (16)

WEATHERSFIELD WINDSOR MANUFACTORY. Weathersfield, Vermont, c. 1825. (6)

WELLS, JOHN I. Hartford, Connecticut, 1798–1807. (1; *Connecticut Courant,* 19 February 1798)

WELLS, JOHN I., and FLINT, ERASTUS. Hartford, Connecticut, 1807–1812. (1)

WEST, THOMAS. New London, Connecticut, 1815–1828. (1; *New London Gazette,* 26 April 1815)

WEST, THOMAS, and DAVID, S. New London, Connecticut, 1807. (18)

WETHERBEE, A[BIJAH] (1781–1835). New Ipswich, New Hampshire, 1813–1835. Was in partnership with Peter Wilder, Josiah Prescott Wilder, and John B. Wilder. (7)

WEYMOUTH, E. Maine, c. 1825–1840. (*Newtown Bee,* 26 August 1983)

WHITAKER, JAMES. Philadelphia, 1800–1820. Worked at 19 and 33 Dock St., 70 Spruce St., and 26 Lombard St.; also made fancy chairs. (16)

WHITAKER and NEWCOMB. Bridgeton, New Jersey, 1856. (11)

WHITE, SAMUEL K. Exeter, Maine, nineteenth century. (17)

WHITE, WILLIAM. *See* HUBBARD and WHITE

WHITELOCK. *See* LOVE and WHITELOCK

WICKERSHAM. *See* BURCHALL and WICKERSHAM

WIDDIFIELD (WIDDEFIELD, WIDOWFIELD), WILLIAM (d. 1822). Philadelphia, 1768–1779. A branded Widdifield chair is in the collection of Independence National Historical Park. (5; 8; 17)
A. Label of William Widdifield.
B. Brand of William Widdifield.

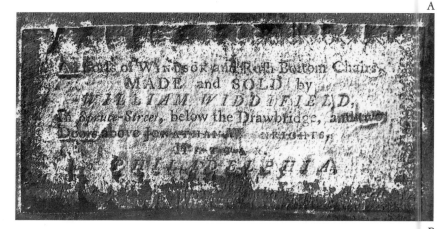

A

B

WILDER, JOHN B. *See* WETHERBEE, A.

WILDER, J[OSIAH] [PRESCOTT] (1787–1825). New Ipswich, New Hampshire, c. 1807. (7; 13:May 1979) *See also* WETHERBEE, A.

WILDER, PETER. *See* WEATHERBEE, A.

WILES, WILLIAM W. Lebanon, Ohio, 1831. (17)

WILLIAMS, EBENEZER. East Windsor, Connecticut, 1790. Worked in the shop of Eliphalet Chapin. (17; *Connecticut Courant,* 3 May 1790; "A Selection of Nineteenth-Century American Chairs," Stowe-Day Foundation, 1973)

WILLIS, JOHN. Philadelphia, 1792–1811. (16)

WILSON, E. H. Wooster, Ohio, 1820–1850. (17)

WILSON, H. A. Wooster, Ohio, 1820–1850. (17)

WING, SAMUEL (1774–1854). Sandwich, Massachusetts, 1800?–1854. Made a wide variety of furniture; Wing chairs are in the collection of Old Sturbridge Village. (13:May 1968)

WIRE, I. [JOHN]. Philadelphia, 1791–1813. Worked at 207 and 109 S. Front St. and 208 S. Water St.; made chairs for Governor John Penn. (5; 16; 17)

WOOD, N. F. Philadelphia, 1852. (11)

WORREL and MORRIS. Pennsylvania?, c. 1800–1810. (18)

Y

YATES, J. New York City?, c. 1790. (6)

YOUNG, GEORGE. Wilmington, Delaware, 1800. Worked in partnership with Samuel Nichols. (2)

Z

ZUTPHEN, W. Pennsylvania?, c. 1800. A Zutphen chair is in the collection of Colonial Williamsburg. (18)

Notes

1. A very rare example of a stylish low-back made during this period is shown as figure 64 in *The Windsor Style in America* by Charles Santore (Philadelphia: Running Press, 1981), p. 80.

2. For an example of a typical English armchair in the High Wickham style, see *The Windsor Style,* p. 39, figure 11.

3. An example of the English design is pictured as figure 80 of *The Windsor Style,* p. 89.

4. For a chair of related design, see *The Windsor Style,* p. 109, figure 118.

5. An armchair version of this side chair, one produced in the same region during the same period, is pictured as figure 151 of *The Windsor Style,* p. 129.

6. Patricia E. Kane, "Samuel Gragg: His Bentwood Fancy Chairs," *Yale University Art Gallery Bulletin,* V. 33, No. 2, Autumn, 1971, p. 28.

7. Ibid.

8. Ibid., *29.*

9. Ibid.

10. Three other examples from the New York area are shown in *The Windsor Style* as figures 134 and 135, p. 120, and figure 235, p. 177.

11. Ethel Hall Bjerkoe, *The Cabinetmakers of America* (New York: Doubleday & Company, 1957), p. 31.

12. See *The Windsor Style in America,* p. 115, figure 128.

13. Robert Bishop, *The American Chair, 1640–1970* (New York: E. P. Dutton, Inc., 1972), p. 267.

14. Nancy Goyne Evans, "Fancy Windsor Chairs of the 1790s," *The Newtown* (Pa.) *Bee,* November 6, 1981, p. 66.

15. For a similar chair with Tracy's brand, see *The Windsor Style,* p. 112, figure 121.

16. Ibid., 51. This attribution is based upon the chair shown in color plate V.

17. Ibid., p. 140, figure 170.

18. Ibid., p. 153, figure 190. The design of this settee is virtually identical to one that bears Tracy's brand, with the exception of the crest rail.

19. Ibid., p. 129, figure 151. The shape of the arms, seat, medial stretcher, and the swellings at the ends of the side stretchers of figure 232 are similar to those of the Maryland armchair pictured.

20. Ibid., 182, figure 244.

Index

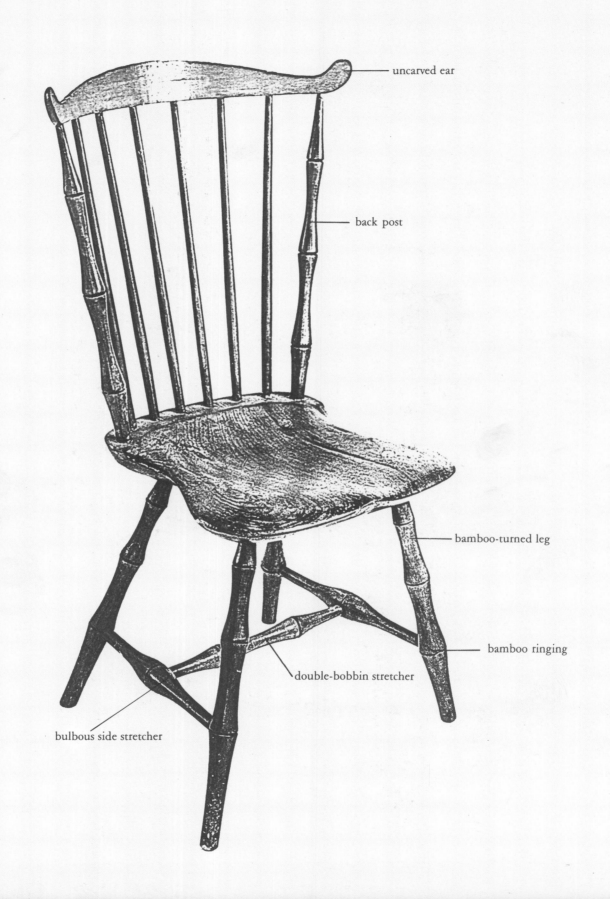

uncarved ear

back post

bamboo-turned leg

bamboo ringing

double-bobbin stretcher

bulbous side stretcher